Math
made easy

Grade 1
ages 6-7
Workbook

Author
Sue Phillips

Consultant
Sean McArdle

LONDON • NEW YORK • SYDNEY • MOSCOW • DELHI

Numbers

Trace the numbers.

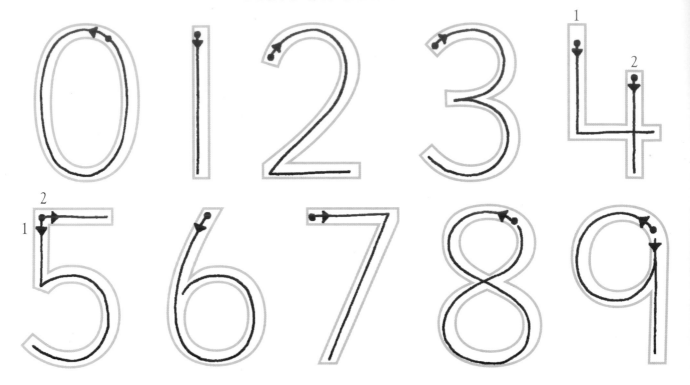

Write the numbers.

Progress Chart

This chart lists the topics in the book. Once you have completed each page, stick a star in the correct box below.

Page	Topic	Star	Page	Topic	Star	Page	Topic	Star
2	Numbers	★	13	Finding 10s	★	24	Subtracting	★
3	Numbers and pictures	★	14	Tens and ones	★	25	Counting back	★
4	Counting	★	15	One more or one less?	★	26	Sets	★
5	Counting out loud	★	16	Ordering	★	27	Money	★
6	Missing numbers	★	17	More than or less than?	★	28	Ordering stories	★
7	Making 10	★	18	Greater or less?	★	29	Time	★
8	Count by 10s	★	19	Comparing	★	30	Graphs	★
9	Count by 2s	★	20	Halves	★	31	2-dimensional shapes	★
10	Patterns	★	21	Quarters	★	32	3-dimensional shapes	★
11	Adding machines	★	22	Adding up	★	33	Writing numbers	★
12	Reading numbers	★	23	Adding animals	★	34	Counting	★

0	1	2	3	4	5	6	7	8	9	10
zero	one	two	three	four	five	six	seven	eight	nine	ten

When you have completed the progress chart in this book, fill in the certificate at the back.

Numbers and pictures

Count the animals, draw the dots, and write the number.

| 2 | two |

Draw your own examples.

Counting

Connect each set to the correct number.

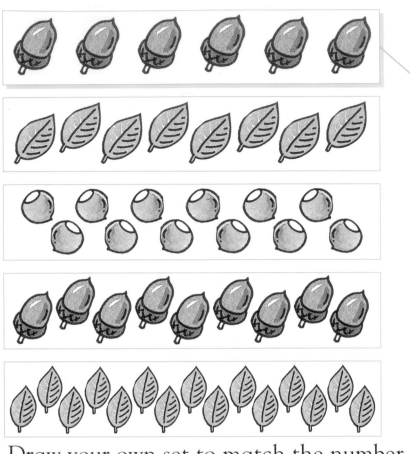

 8

 9

 6

15

 10

Draw your own set to match the number.

 12

Count the beads.

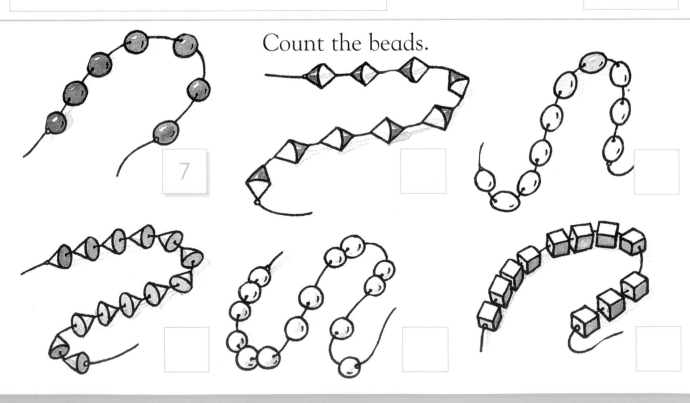

7

Counting out loud

Say and write the missing numbers.

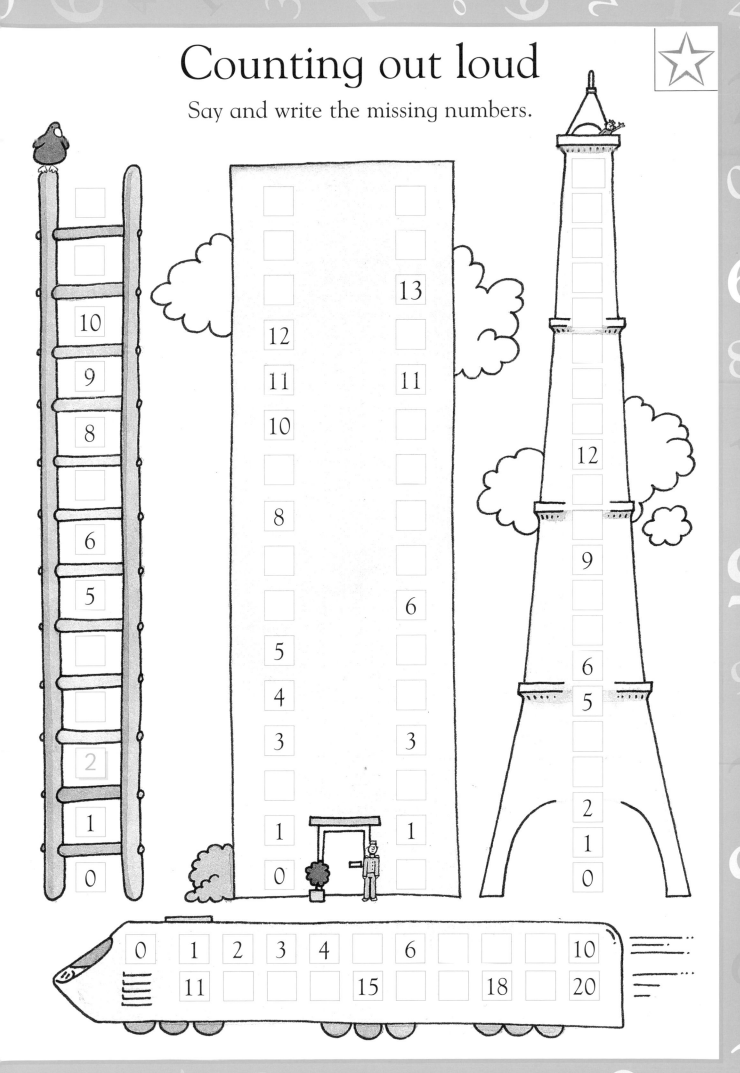

Missing numbers

Write in the missing numbers.

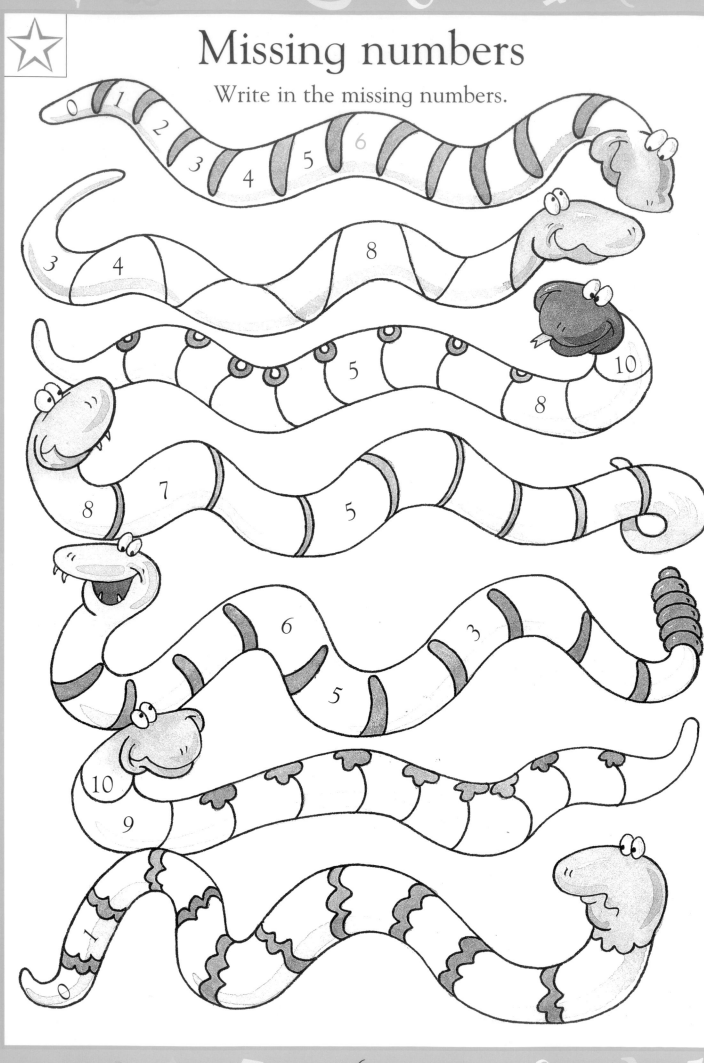

Making 10

Color some fish green, and write the correct numbers in the boxes.

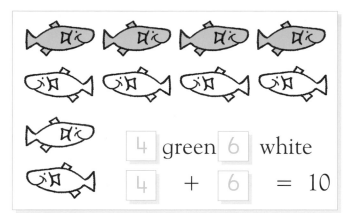

4 green 6 white

4 + 6 = 10

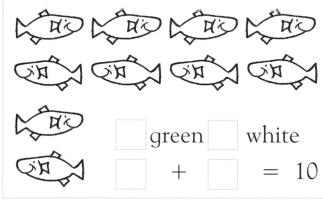

green white

+ = 10

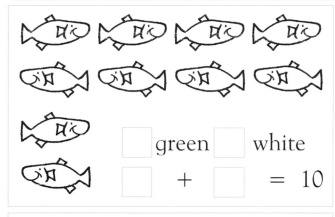

green white

+ = 10

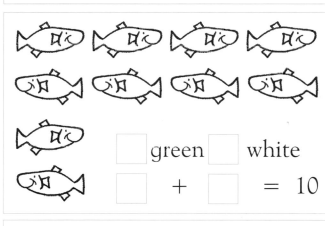

green white

+ = 10

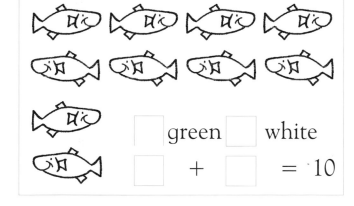

green white

+ = 10

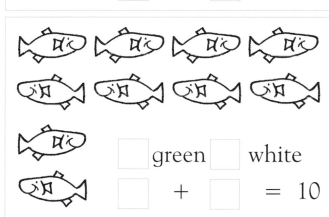

green white

+ = 10

Write the missing numbers in the boxes to make 10.

10 + 0 = 10   6 + = 10   2 + = 10

9 + = 10   5 + = 10   1 + = 10

8 + = 10   4 + = 10   0 + = 10

7 + = 10   3 + = 10

Count by 10s

Match the numbers to the words.

fifty	ten	thirty	twenty	forty

10	20	30	40	50	60	70	80	90	100

seventy	ninety	sixty	eighty	one hundred

Which numbers has the snail hidden?

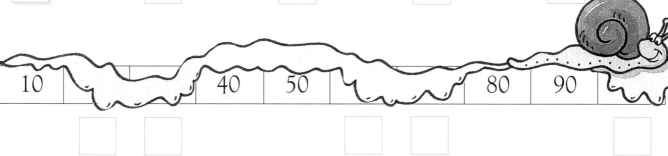

| | 20 | | 40 | | 60 | | 80 | | 100 |

| 10 | | | | |

| 10 | | 40 | 50 | | | 80 | 90 | |

Help the snail follow the bricks in the right order.

0	62	36	11	25	57	3	44	58	22
10	20	72	61	60	70	80	73	43
89	68	30	40	50	88	32	90	69	9
75	23	54	24	24	74	92	100	14

Count by 2s

Fill in the "hops" and circle the even numbers.

Color the even numbers.

1	2	3	4	5
6	7	8	9	10
11	12	13	14	15
16	17	18	19	20
21	22	23	24	25
26	27	28	29	30

Connect the dots in order.

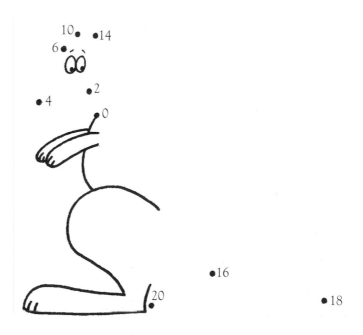

Patterns

Continue the pattern.

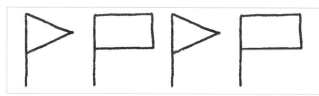

Make your own patterns.

Continue the number patterns.

2	4	6	2	4	6	2	4	6			
10	9	9	10	9							
1	3	5	7	1							
5	5	5	6	5							

Adding machines

Add the numbers, and write the answers.

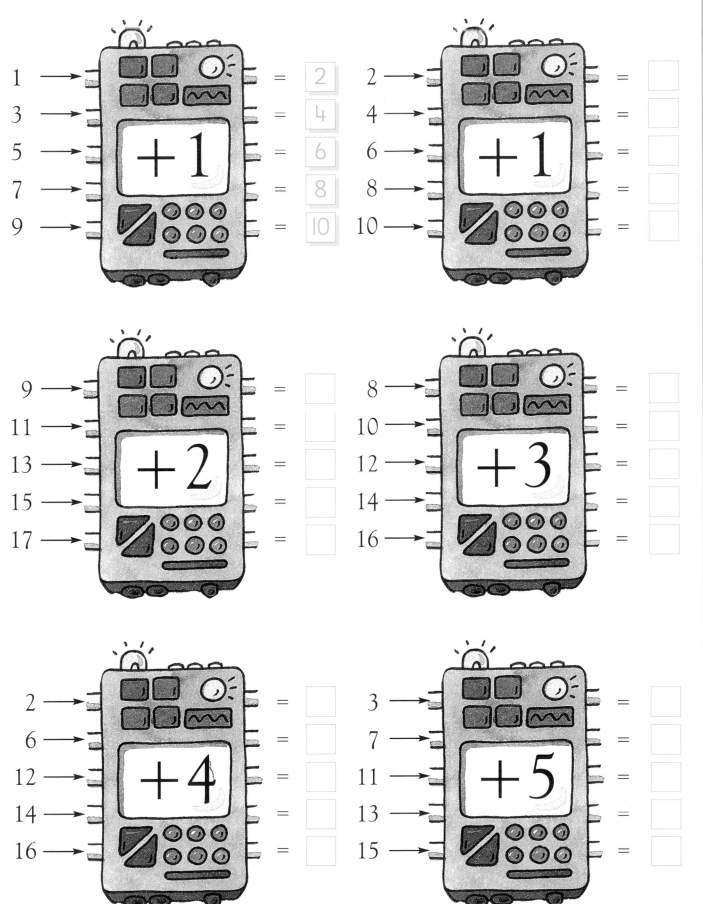

Machine 1 (+1):
- 1 = 2
- 3 = 4
- 5 = 6
- 7 = 8
- 9 = 10

Machine 2 (+1):
- 2 =
- 4 =
- 6 =
- 8 =
- 10 =

Machine 3 (+2):
- 9 =
- 11 =
- 13 =
- 15 =
- 17 =

Machine 4 (+3):
- 8 =
- 10 =
- 12 =
- 14 =
- 16 =

Machine 5 (+4):
- 2 =
- 6 =
- 12 =
- 14 =
- 16 =

Machine 6 (+5):
- 3 =
- 7 =
- 11 =
- 13 =
- 15 =

Reading numbers

Color enough things to match the number in each box.

12

10
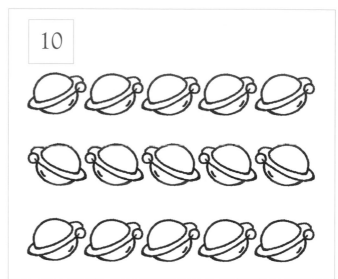

9

7

Draw your own example.

11

Finding 10s

Ring 10 items, and write the numbers.

12 = 10 + 2

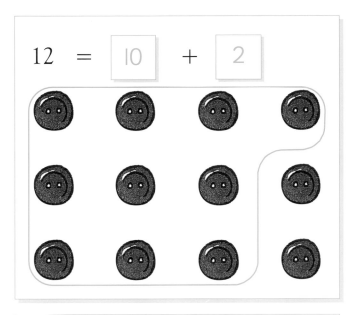

16 = [ ] + [ ]

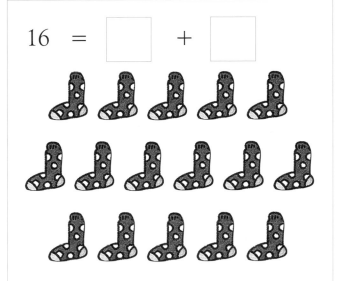

19 = [ ] + [ ]

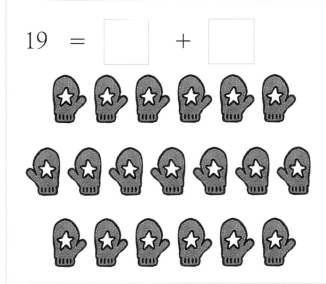

17 = [ ] + [ ]

11 = [ ] + [ ]

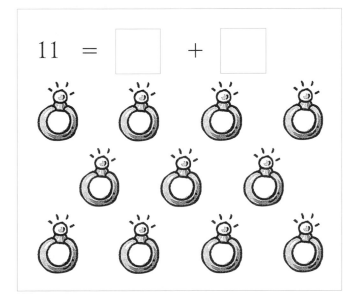

20 = [ ] + [ ]

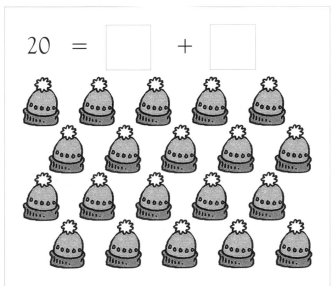

Tens and ones

How many tens and ones do you see?

tens	ones	tens	ones	tens	ones
1	4				

14

tens	ones	tens	ones	tens	ones

Draw the tens and ones.

tens	ones	tens	ones	tens	ones
1	9	1	5		3

19

14

One more or one less?

Write one less and one more than the numbers shown in the boxes.

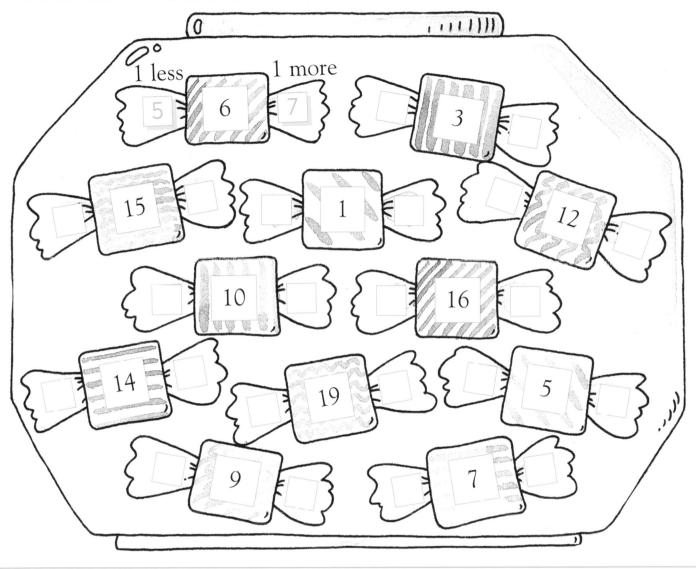

Draw one more or one less, and write the new number.

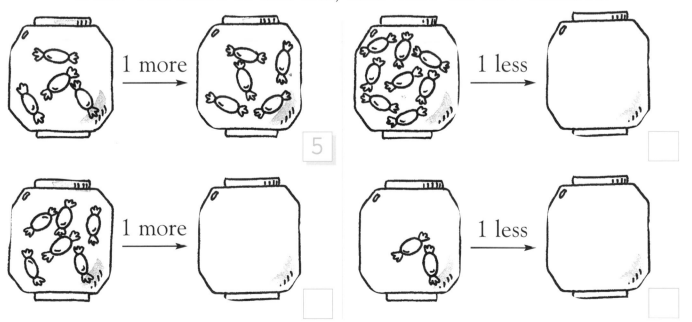

15

Ordering

Color the prize ribbons.

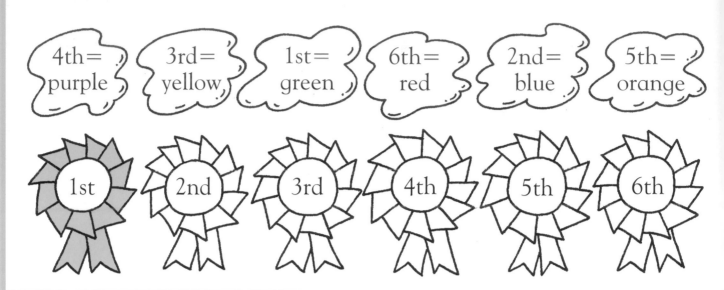

4th = purple 3rd = yellow 1st = green 6th = red 2nd = blue 5th = orange

1st 2nd 3rd 4th 5th 6th

Which rabbit is 1st, 2nd, 3rd ...?

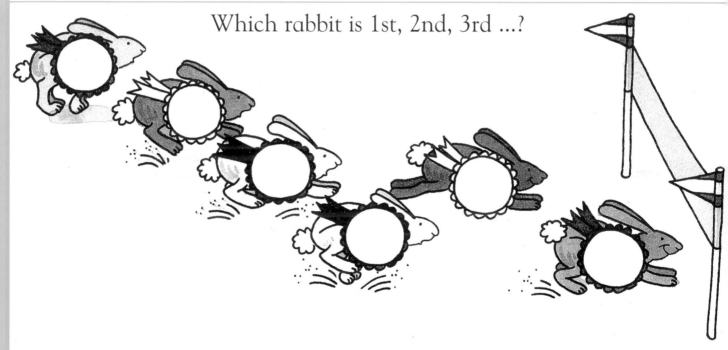

Which shape comes 1st, 2nd, 3rd ...?

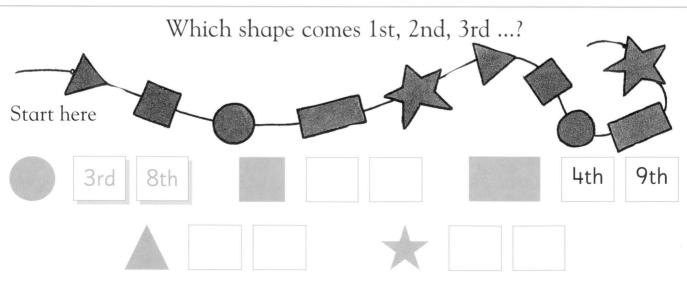

Start here

3rd   8th   4th   9th

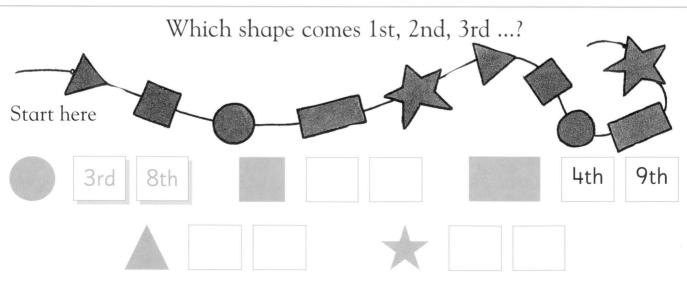

More than or less than?

Fill in the apples and numbers that make each sentence true.

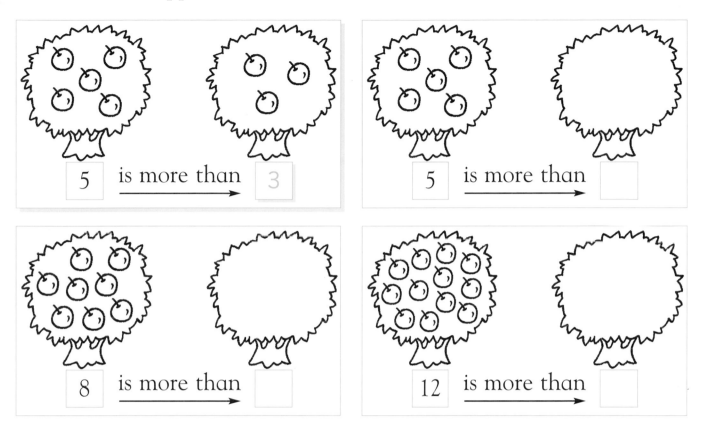

| 5 | is more than → | 3 |

| 5 | is more than → | |

| 8 | is more than → | |

| 12 | is more than → | |

Fill in the flowers and numbers that make each sentence true.

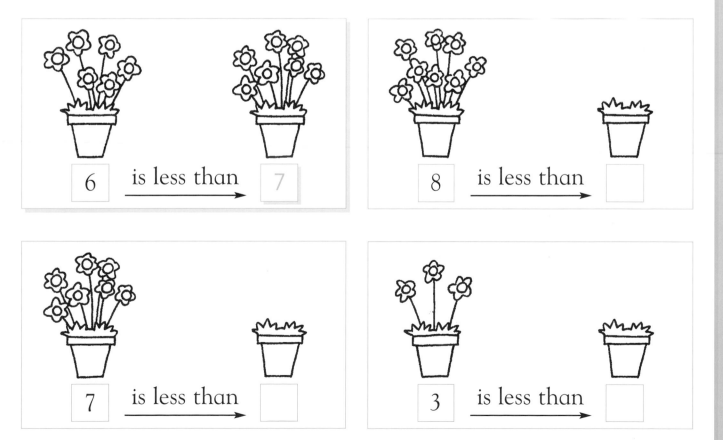

| 6 | is less than → | 7 |

| 8 | is less than → | |

| 7 | is less than → | |

| 3 | is less than → | |

Greater or less?

Draw the hungry crocodiles.
They always eat the greater numbers!

6 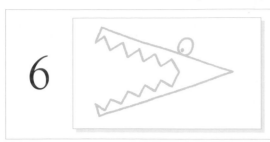 4

2 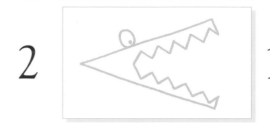 12

5 10

3 13

8 13

6 16

15 9

15 20

10 2

11 12

20 10

1 0

Comparing

heavier   lighter   bigger   smaller   longer   shorter

Draw the pictures to make each comparison true.

Halves

Color one half ($\frac{1}{2}$) of each shape.

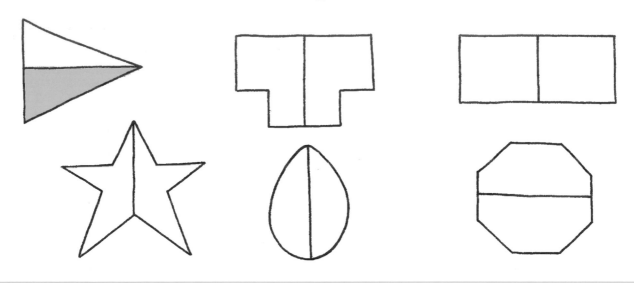

Write a ✓ in the box if $\frac{1}{2}$ the figure is shaded and a ✗ if less than $\frac{1}{2}$ is shaded.

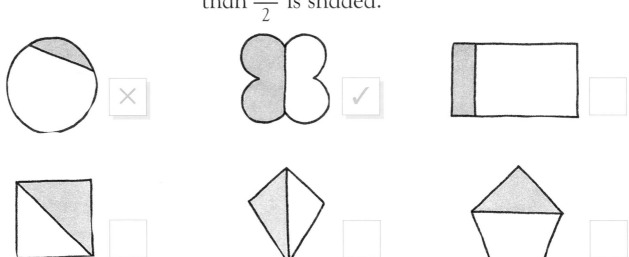

Color one half ($\frac{1}{2}$) of each figure.

Quarters

Color one quarter ($\frac{1}{4}$) of each shape.

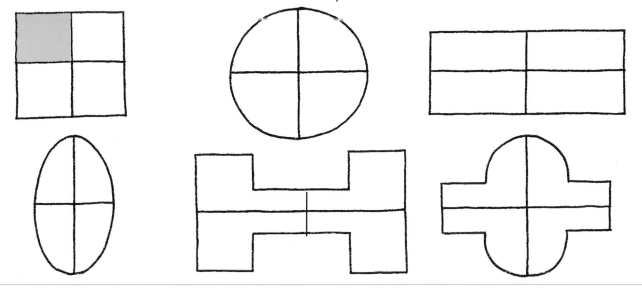

Write a ✔ in the box if $\frac{1}{4}$ of the figure is shaded and a ✗ if less than $\frac{1}{4}$ is shaded.

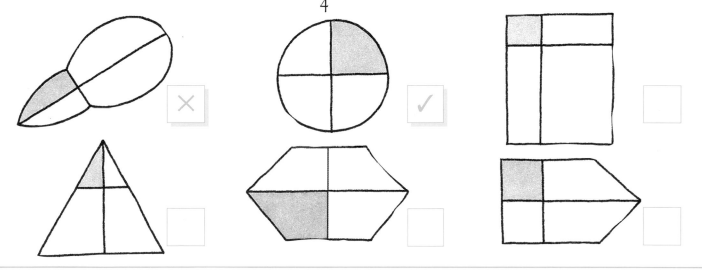

✗ ✔

Color one quarter ($\frac{1}{4}$) of each picture.

Adding up

Fill in the missing numbers, and add.

 3 + 3 = 6

 4 + 4 = ☐

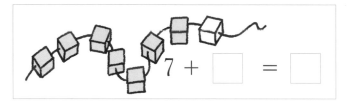 7 + ☐ = ☐

 6 + ☐ = ☐

 3 + ☐ = ☐

☐ + ☐ = 15

Count on to find out on which step the rabbit stops.

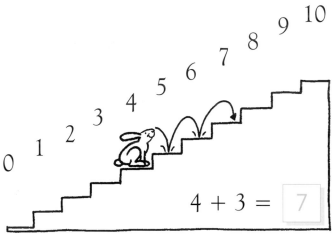 4 + 3 = 7

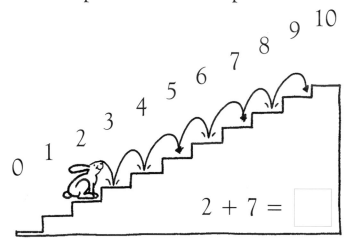 2 + 7 = ☐

 8 + 2 = ☐

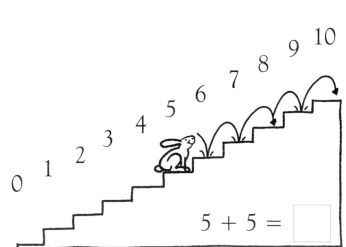 5 + 5 = ☐

Adding animals

Count and add the animals, and then write the new number.

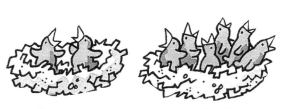  

2 + 6 = 8   ☐ + ☐ = ☐

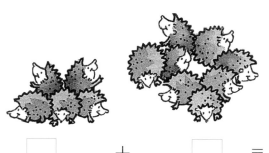 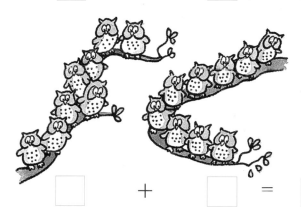

☐ + ☐ = ☐   ☐ + ☐ = ☐

    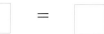

☐ + ☐ = ☐   ☐ + ☐ = ☐

Fill in the missing numbers in the equations.

7 + 4 = 11   3 + ☐ = 12   6 + 6 = ☐

9 + 5 = ☐   2 + 8 = ☐   3 + 11 = ☐

9 + 3 = ☐   6 + ☐ = 10   13 + ☐ = 17

2 + ☐ = 5   16 + ☐ = 16   15 + ☐ = 19

23

Subtracting

Cross out the correct number of animals, and fill in the answers.

$4 - 1 =$ | 3

$6 - 2 =$ |

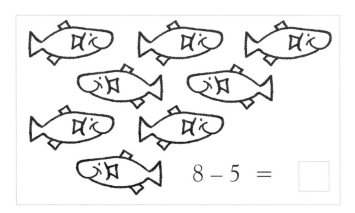

$8 - 5 =$ |

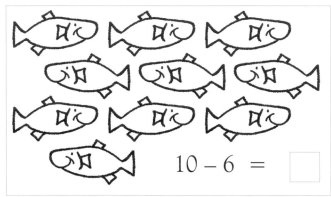

$10 - 6 =$ |

Cross out the correct number of fruits, and fill in the answers.

$8 - 3 =$ |

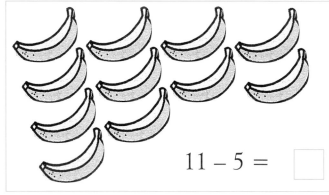

$11 - 5 =$ |

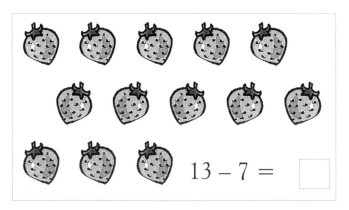

$13 - 7 =$ |

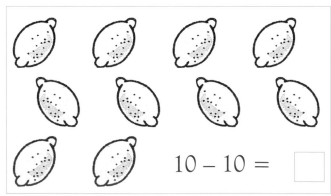

$10 - 10 =$ |

Counting back

Count back to find out on which step the frog stops.

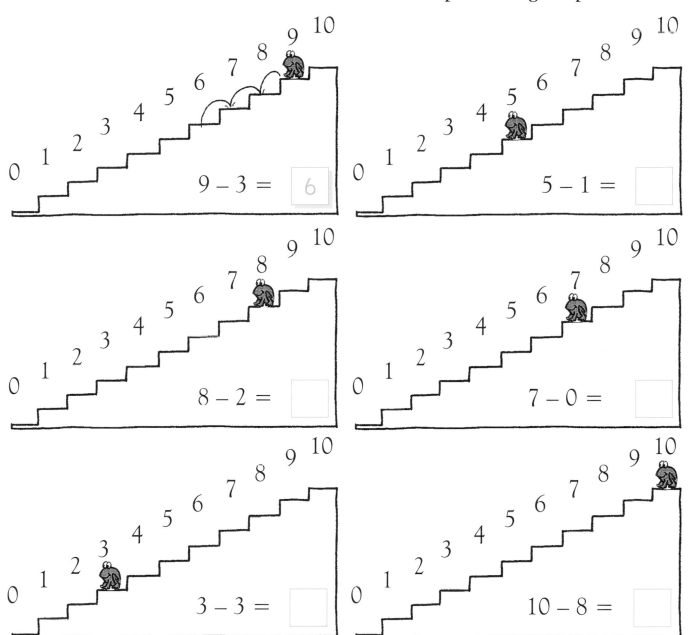

$9 - 3 = \boxed{6}$

$5 - 1 = \boxed{}$

$8 - 2 = \boxed{}$

$7 - 0 = \boxed{}$

$3 - 3 = \boxed{}$

$10 - 8 = \boxed{}$

Write the missing numbers in the boxes.

$3 - 3 = \boxed{0}$ $20 - 10 = \boxed{}$ $9 - \boxed{} = 6$ $15 - \boxed{} = 5$

$5 - 4 = \boxed{}$ $8 - 8 = \boxed{}$ $5 - \boxed{} = 0$ $20 - \boxed{} = 4$

$15 - 4 = \boxed{}$ $19 - 9 = \boxed{}$ $6 - \boxed{} = 2$ $18 - \boxed{} = 11$

$10 - 9 = \boxed{}$ $16 - 9 = \boxed{}$ $10 - \boxed{} = 4$ $13 - \boxed{} = 10$

Sets

Write the missing numbers in the boxes.

  2 sets of 3 = 6

  2 sets of 5 = [ ]

   3 sets of 4 = [ ]

   [ ] sets of 2 = [ ]

[ ] sets of 2 = [ ]

Draw pictures in the boxes to match the equations.

  3 sets of 3 = 9

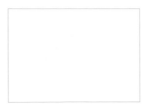 2 sets of 4 = 8

26

Money

Which coin?

|  Penny |  Nickel |  Dime |  Quarter |

How much?

3¢

Put the correct change in the piggy bank.

3¢   11¢   7¢

Ordering stories

Which happens 1st, 2nd, and 3rd?

  2nd

 3rd

1st

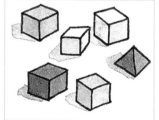

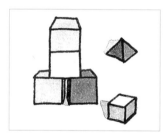

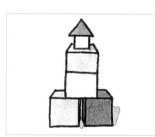

Match the pictures to the order in which they happened.

| 4th | 2nd | 1st | 3rd |

Time

Write the time in each box.

| 3 | o'clock | | o'clock | | o'clock | | o'clock |

Draw the hands on the clock faces.

4 o'clock   10 o'clock   1 o'clock   6 o'clock

Match the times to the clocks.

| 12 o'clock | 7 o'clock | 2 o'clock | 9 o'clock |

Graphs

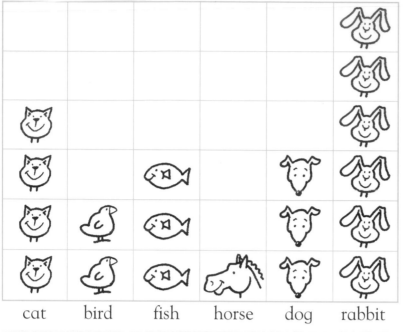

					rabbit
					rabbit
cat					rabbit
cat		fish		dog	rabbit
cat	bird	fish		dog	rabbit
cat	bird	fish	horse	dog	rabbit
cat	bird	fish	horse	dog	rabbit

Number of pets

Pets

How many pets?

Draw the pet that matches the number.

6 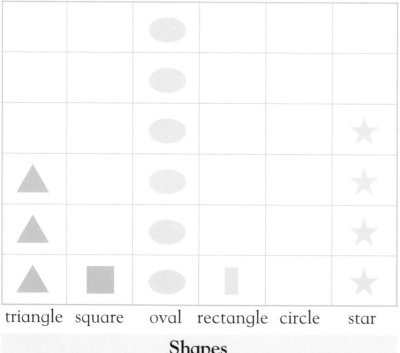   2 [ ]   1 [ ]

Number of shapes

triangle	square	oval	rectangle	circle	star

Shapes

How many shapes?

Which shape matches each number?

4 [ ]   0 [ ]   3 [ ]

2-dimensional shapes

| | = yellow | = green | = purple | = blue |

Color the shapes.

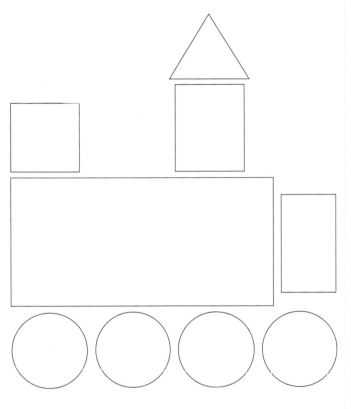

How many?

      ○   ▯

Color the shapes.

How many?

△   ○   ▯

Draw a picture using the shapes shown on this page.

How many?

3-dimensional shapes

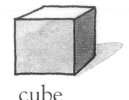 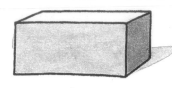 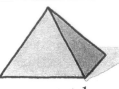

| cube | prism | sphere | pyramid |

Match the shapes to the names.

   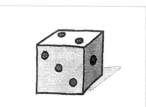

| pyramid | sphere | cube | prism |

How many?

How many?

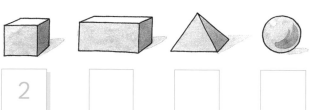

| 2 | | | | | | | | |

Writing numbers

Count, write, and say the number of letters.

Christina — 9 — nine

Tarik —

Grandpa —

Happy Birthday —

Good Morning Everyone —

How are you today? —

Write your name.

Make up your own message.

33

Counting

Write the missing numbers.

Counting on by 2s

Hop by 2s. Color the squares.

Elizabeth Even

Oliver Odd

0	1	2	3	4	5	6	7	8
17	16	15	14	13	12	11	10	9

0		2	3	4	5	6	7	8
17	16	15	14	13	12	11	10	9

What letters will you find? Say the numbers as you draw.

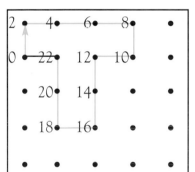

Even numbers
2   4   6   8

Odd numbers
1   3   5

Write the numbers.

Even numbers

2   4   6   8 ☐ ☐ ☐ ☐ ☐ ☐

Odd numbers

1   3   5   ☐ ☐ ☐ ☐ ☐ ☐

Most and least

Circle the set with the most items in it.

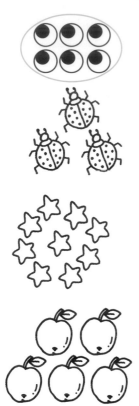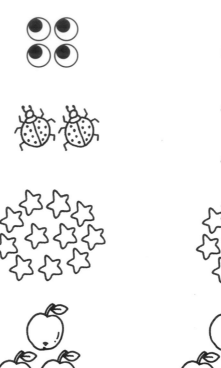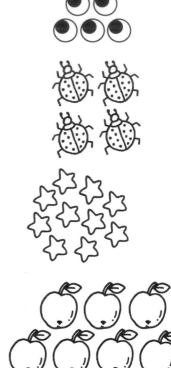

Circle the set with the least items in it.

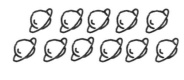

Counting by 10s

Use this number line to help you.

0	10	20	30	40	50	60	70	80	90	100
zero	ten	twenty	thirty	forty	fifty	sixty	seventy	eighty	ninety	one hundred

How many candies? Count, say, and write.

30 thirty

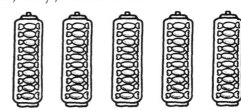

50

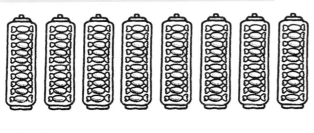

☐ eighty

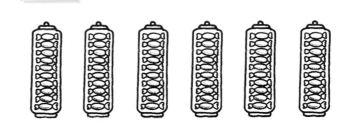

60

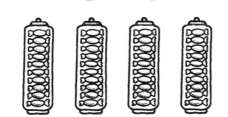

☐

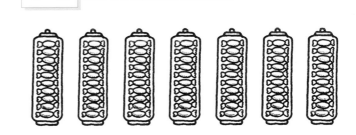

☐

Put the numbers in the right order.

10   60   100   50   20   70   90   30   40   80

10 20

Greatest first

100 90 80

37

Counting forward or back

Draw pathways by writing the missing numbers.

Reading numbers

Connect the numbers, and complete the drawings.

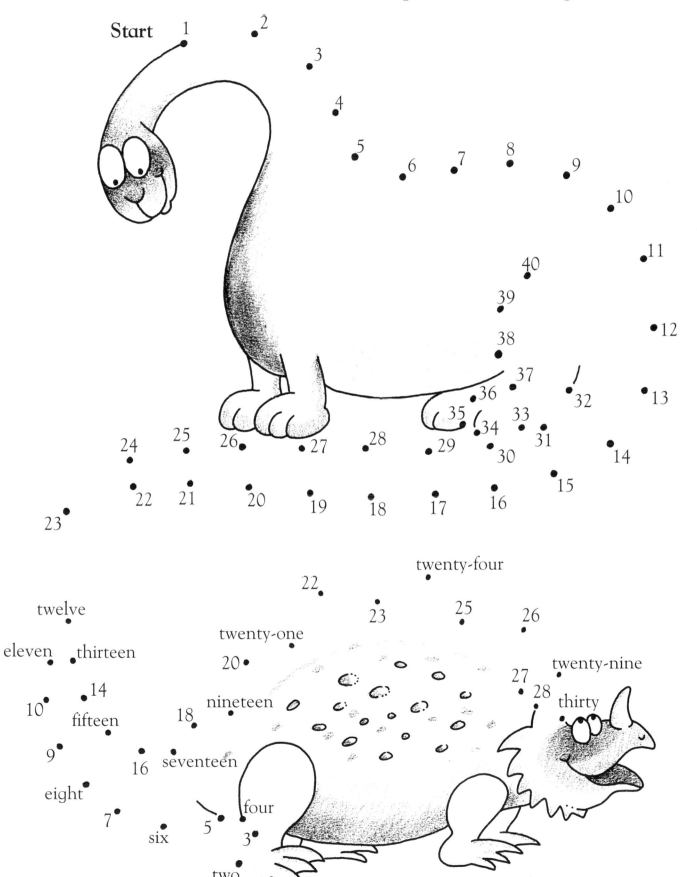

Start 1 2
3
4
5 6 7 8 9
10
11
40
39 12
38
37
36 32 13
35 33
34 31
24 25 26 27 28 29 30 14
15
22 21 20 19 18 17 16
23

twenty-four
22
twelve 23 25 26
eleven thirteen twenty-one
20
14 twenty-nine
10 fifteen 18 nineteen 27 28
9 16 seventeen thirty
eight four
7 5
six 3
two 1 **Start**

Tens and ones

Write the tens and ones.

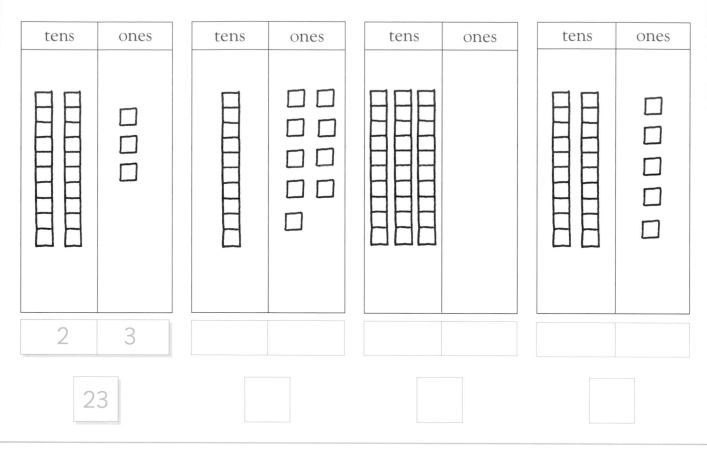

tens	ones
2	3

23

tens	ones

tens	ones

tens	ones

Draw and write the tens and ones.

tens	ones

29

tens	ones

34

Comparisons

Add the values, and write *is greater than* or *is less than*.

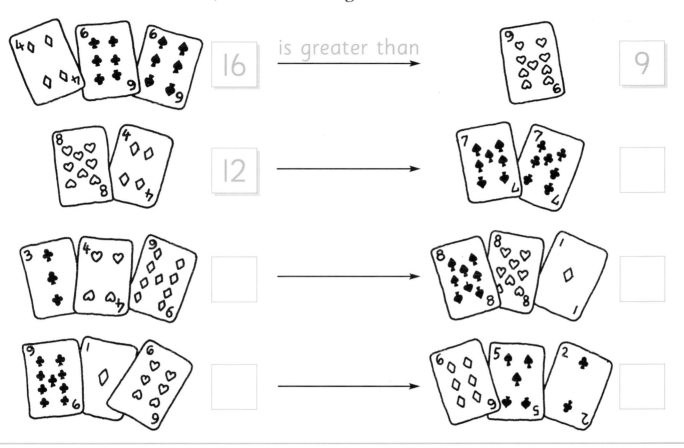

Write the numbers that are 1 more, 1 less, or between.

1 less	between	1 more
20	21	22

1 less	number	1 more
	26	

number	between	number
19		21

1 less	number	1 more
	29	

1 less	number	1 more
	11	

number	between	number
30		32

Comparing money

Color the one who has the most money.

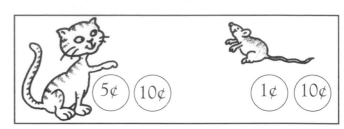

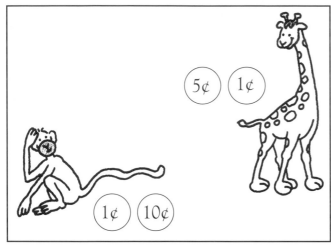

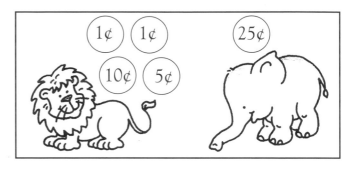

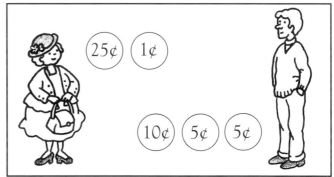

Draw some coins in the purses.

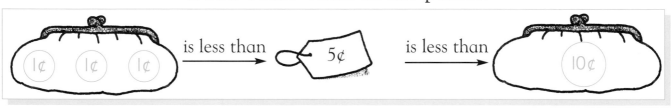

is less than   5¢   is less than

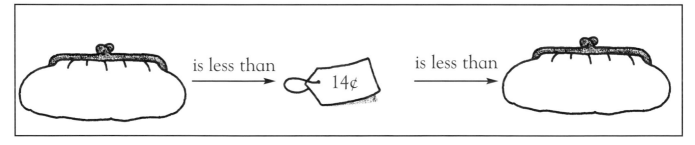

is less than   14¢   is less than

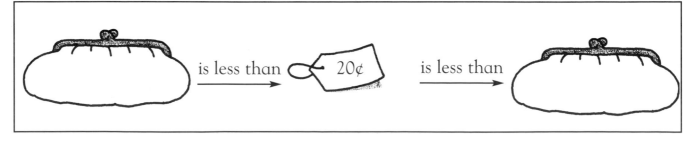

is less than   20¢   is less than

Spot the doubles

Draw the missing spots and write the numbers.

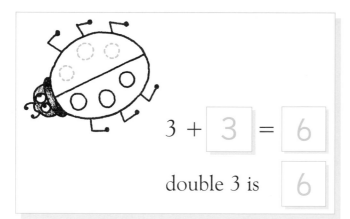

$3 + \boxed{3} = \boxed{6}$

double 3 is $\boxed{6}$

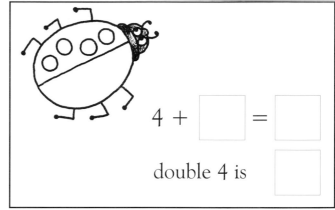

$4 + \boxed{} = \boxed{}$

double 4 is $\boxed{}$

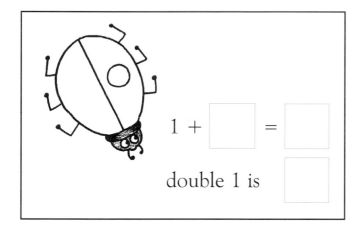

$1 + \boxed{} = \boxed{}$

double 1 is $\boxed{}$

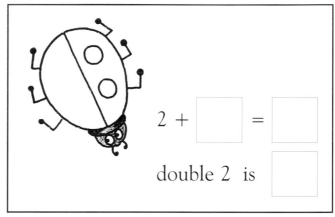

$2 + \boxed{} = \boxed{}$

double 2 is $\boxed{}$

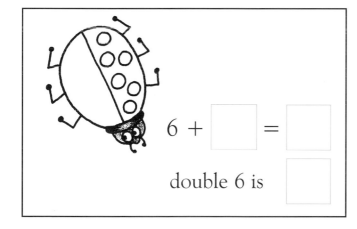

$6 + \boxed{} = \boxed{}$

double 6 is $\boxed{}$

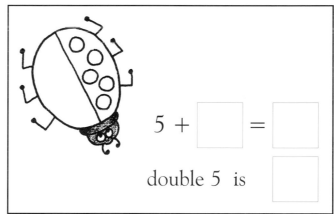

$5 + \boxed{} = \boxed{}$

double 5 is $\boxed{}$

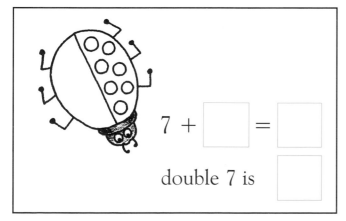

$7 + \boxed{} = \boxed{}$

double 7 is $\boxed{}$

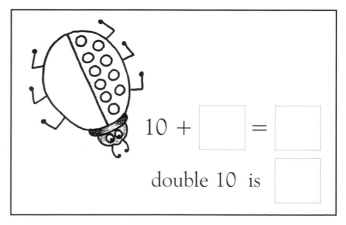

$10 + \boxed{} = \boxed{}$

double 10 is $\boxed{}$

10 more or 10 less

Draw a line to add 10 to each number on the rocket.

Draw a line to subtract 10 from each number on the rocket.

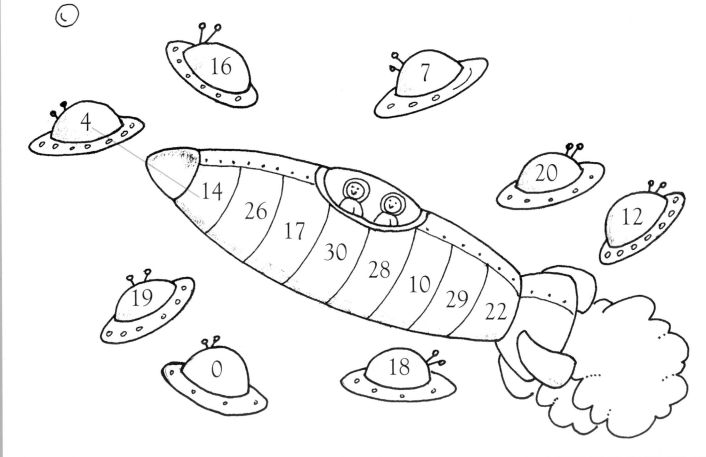

Ordinals

Color the beads.

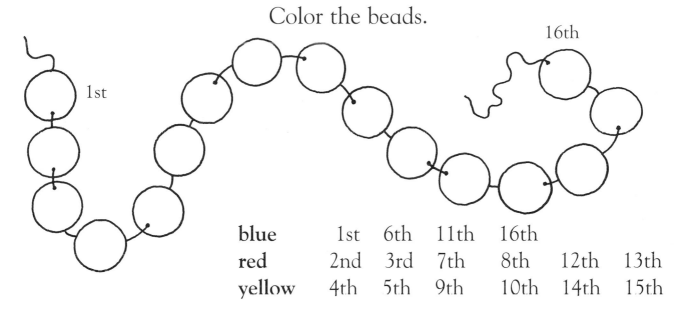

16th

1st

blue	1st	6th	11th	16th		
red	2nd	3rd	7th	8th	12th	13th
yellow	4th	5th	9th	10th	14th	15th

Write the positions.

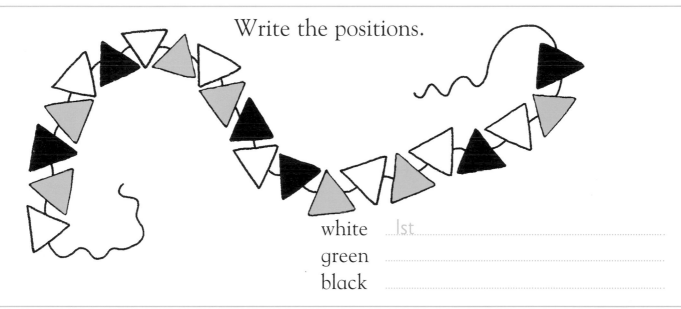

white   1st ....

green   ....

black   ....

Choose 3 colors. Make your own pattern. Write the positions.

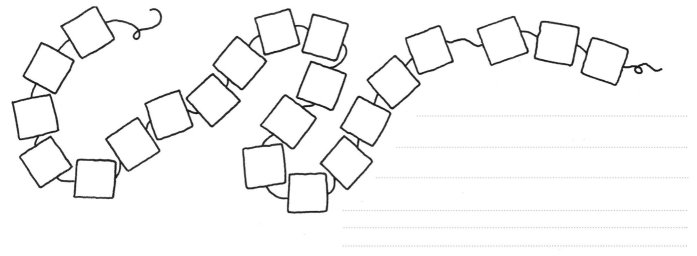

....

....

....

....

....

....

Ordering

Look for a pattern. Write the numbers in order.

10 12 14 16 18

8 7 6 5 4 3

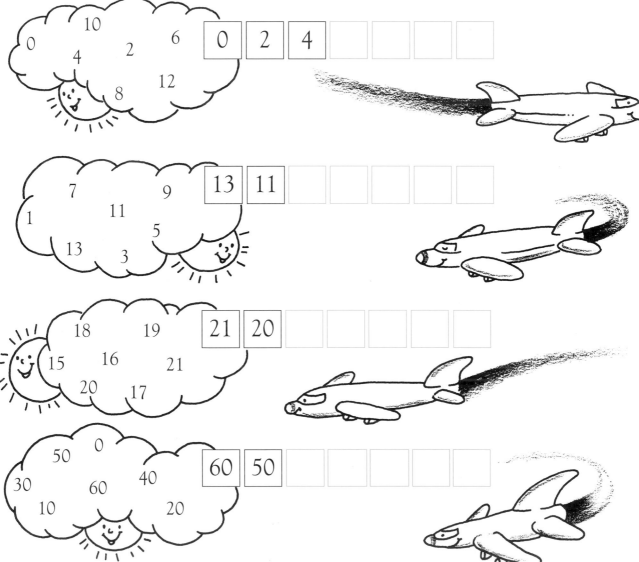

0 2 4

13 11

21 20

60 50

Halves and fourths

For each shape color one half red or one fourth yellow.

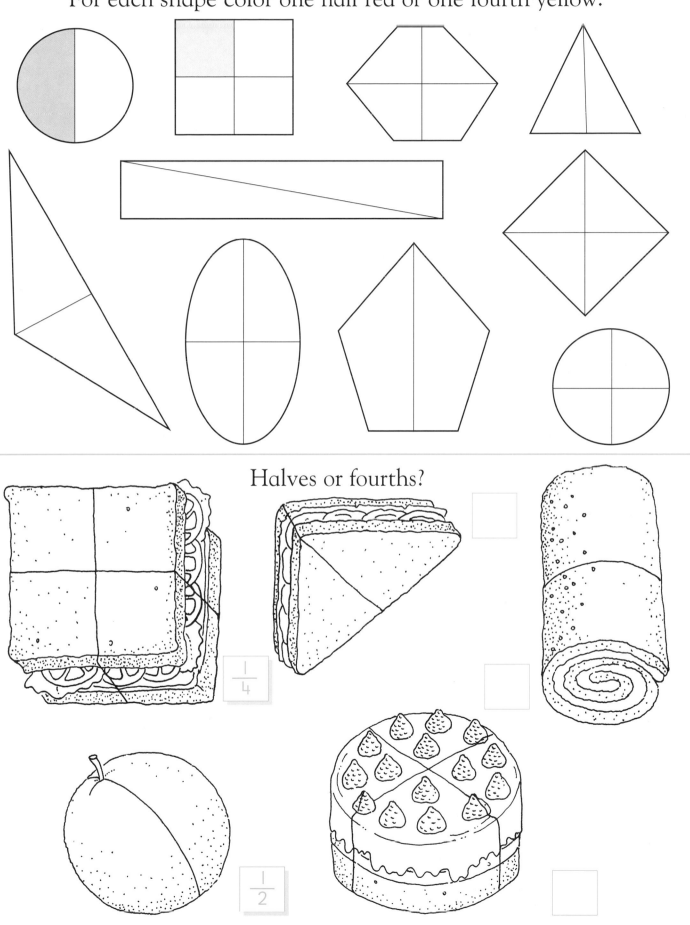

Halves or fourths?

$\frac{1}{4}$

$\frac{1}{2}$

Place value

What is in the ones place in each number?

| 24 | 461 | 87 | 119 |
| 4 | l | | |

| 365 | 68 | 13 | 842 |

What is in the tens place in each number?

| 30 | 594 | 10 | 769 |
| 3 | 9 | | |

| 127 | 81 | 18 | 150 |

What is in the hundreds place in each number?

| 124 | 907 | 436 | 580 |
| l | | | |

Circle the number that has a 7 in the tens place.

457   794   870

Circle the number that has a 3 in the ones place.

134   693   308

Circle the number that has a 1 in the hundreds place.

106   610   421

Expanded form

Write each number as a sum of tens and ones.

54 = 50 + 4   12 =   88 =

47 =   29 =   11 =

75 =   51 =   44 =

62 =   93 =   19 =

25 =   74 =   36 =

Write the missing number.

80 + 6 = 86   90 + 7 = 97

+ 3 = 33   + 1 = 61

10 + = 15   + 8 = 58

20 + = 22   70 + = 79

+ 3 = 43   90 + = 94

Adding dice

Count the dots on the dice.

 + = 9

⚃ + ⚁ = ☐   ⚃ + ⚀ = ☐

⚄ + ⚄ = ☐   ⚄ + ⚅ = ☐

⚀ + ⚀ + ⚂ = ☐   ⚅ + ⚃ + ⚀ = ☐

⚄ + ⚄ + ⚄ = ☐   ⚀ + ⚅ + ⚄ = ☐

Make your own dice problems. You can roll real dice to help.

☐ + ☐ + ☐ + ☐ = ☐

☐ + ☐ + ☐ + ☐ = ☐

☐ + ☐ + ☐ + ☐ = ☐

☐ + ☐ + ☐ + ☐ = ☐

☐ + ☐ + ☐ + ☐ = ☐

Adding

Add up the numbers on the socks.

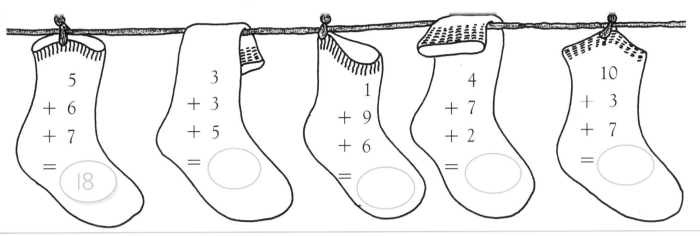

5	3	1	4	10
+ 6	+ 3	+ 9	+ 7	+ 3
+ 7	+ 5	+ 6	+ 2	+ 7
= 18	=	=	=	=

Add up the numbers on the towels.

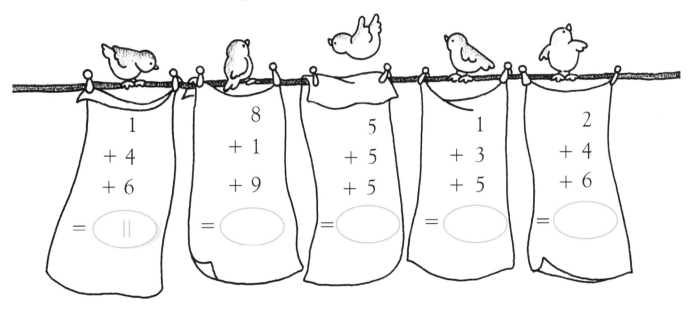

1	8	5	1	2
+ 4	+ 1	+ 5	+ 3	+ 4
+ 6	+ 9	+ 5	+ 5	+ 6
= 11	=	=	=	=

Make up your own number towels.

=   =   =   =   =

Crossing out

Cross out one type of shape in each box.

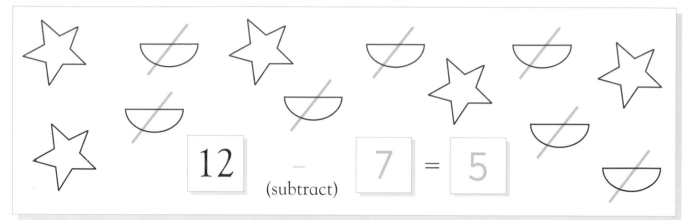

$$12 - 7 = 5$$
(subtract)

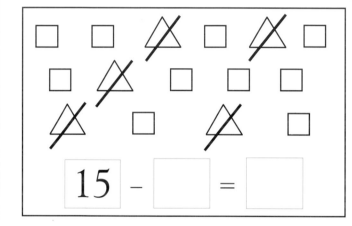

$$15 - \boxed{} = \boxed{}$$

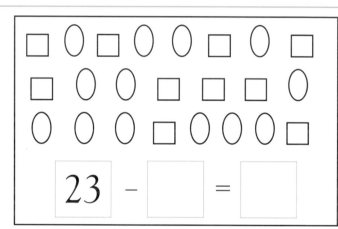

$$23 - \boxed{} = \boxed{}$$

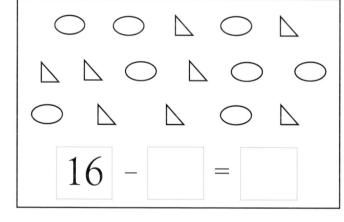

$$16 - \boxed{} = \boxed{}$$

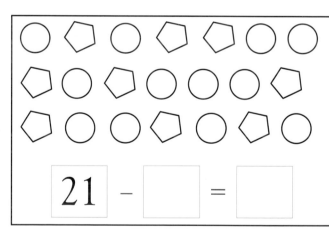

$$21 - \boxed{} = \boxed{}$$

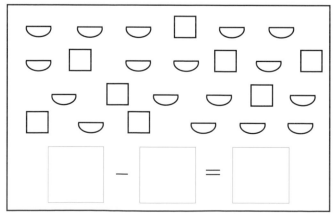

$$\boxed{} - \boxed{} = \boxed{}$$

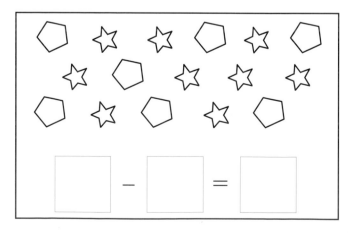

$$\boxed{} - \boxed{} = \boxed{}$$

Subtraction

Say and count as you write.

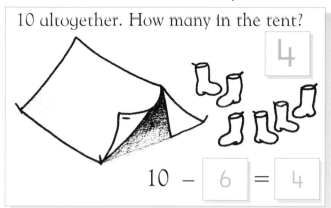

10 altogether. How many in the tent?

4

10 – 6 = 4

18 altogether. How many in the tent?

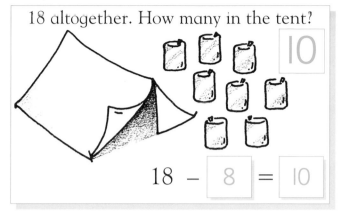

10

18 – 8 = 10

19 altogether. How many in the tent?

19 – □ = □

21 altogether. How many in the tent?

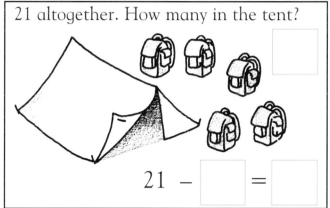

21 – □ = □

Say as you write.

16 – 4 = 12   18 – □ = 7   12 – □ = 2

20 – □ = 14   19 – □ = 5   15 – □ = 9

25 – □ = 4   27 – □ = 11   30 – □ = 10

Say as you write.

15 – 5 = 10   30 – □ = 0   16 – 0 = □

23 – 10 = □   40 – □ = 0   28 – 8 = □

Sets of

Say and count as you write.

$4 + 4 + 4 =$ | 12 | legs

3 | sets of | 4 $\longrightarrow$ 12

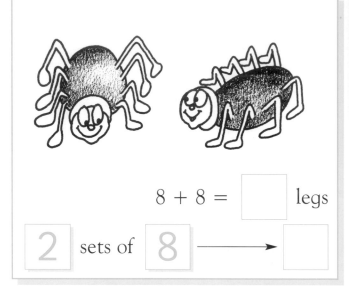

$8 + 8 =$ | ☐ | legs

2 | sets of | 8 $\longrightarrow$ ☐

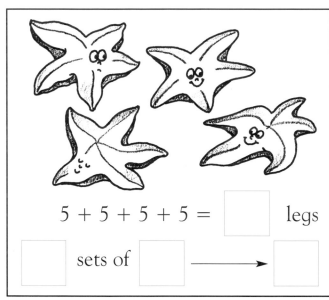

$5 + 5 + 5 + 5 =$ | ☐ | legs

☐ | sets of | ☐ $\longrightarrow$ ☐

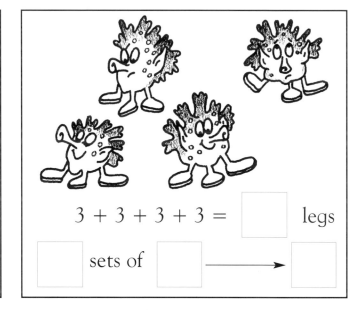

$3 + 3 + 3 + 3 =$ | ☐ | legs

☐ | sets of | ☐ $\longrightarrow$ ☐

$2 + 2 + 2 =$ | ☐ | legs

☐ | sets of | ☐ $\longrightarrow$ ☐

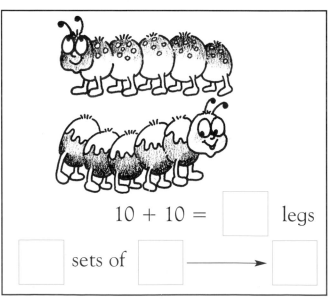

$10 + 10 =$ | ☐ | legs

☐ | sets of | ☐ $\longrightarrow$ ☐

54

Sharing

Share the food equally.

How many each? 2

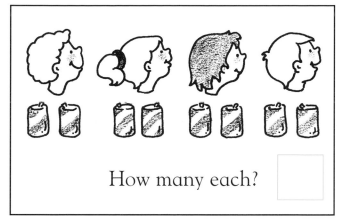

How many each? [ ]

How many each? [ ]

How many each? [ ]

Draw lines to share the picnic.

Addition properties

Write the missing number.

6	+	0	=	6		0	+	6	=	6
	+	7	=	17			+	10	=	17
11	+		=	11			+	11	=	11
4	+		=	12		8	+		=	12
13	+		=	19			+	13	=	19
	+	3	=	3		3	+		=	3

Circle the addition fact that has the same sum as 2 + 3.

1 + 5   (3 + 2)   4 + 2

Circle the addition fact that has the same sum as 5 + 8.

8 + 5   6 + 6   3 + 9

Circle the addition fact that has the same sum as 1 + 7.

8 + 2   2 + 5   7 + 1

Circle the addition fact that has the same sum as 10 + 6.

7 + 4   9 + 9   6 + 10

Circle the addition fact that has the same sum as 4 + 2.

1 + 6   2 + 4   3 + 2

Circle the addition fact that has the same sum as 9 + 5.

5 + 9   7 + 6   10 + 5

Most and least likely

What are you most likely to pick out of each bag? Circle the answer.

What are you least likely to pick out of each bag? Circle the answer.

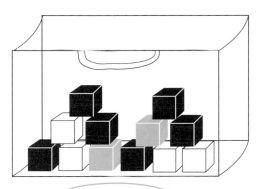

(a black cube)

a gray cube

a white cube

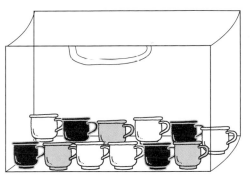

a black tea cup

(a gray tea cup)

a white tea cup

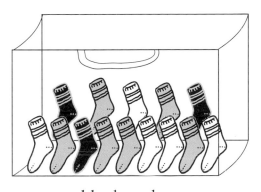

a black sock

a gray sock

a white sock

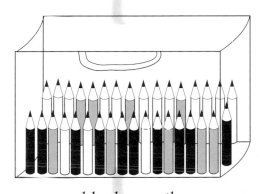

a black pencil

a gray pencil

a white pencil

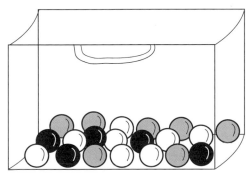

a black marble

a gray marble

a white marble

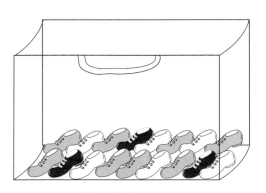

a black boot

a gray boot

a white boot

Days and seasons

Days of the week
Can you write them in order?

Monday Tuesday Wednesday Thursday Friday Saturday Sunday

Wednesday Thursday Fr

Saturday Sunday M

Thursday Friday S

Yesterday and tomorrow

yesterday	today	tomorrow
Tuesday	Wednesday	
	Monday	
	Thursday	
	Sunday	

Seasons of the year
Draw lines to connect each picture to a season.

Spring

Summer

Autumn

Winter

58

Using clocks

Write the time.

8 o'clock

half past 10

Draw the hands.

half past 7

1 o'clock

half past 9

half past 6

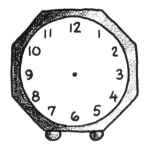
half past 1

11 o'clock

half past 8

2 o'clock

Favorite fruits

This table shows the favorite fruits of a class of children.

grapes	🍇	🍇	🍇					
strawberries	🍓	🍓	🍓	🍓	🍓	🍓	🍓	🍓
bananas	🍌	🍌	🍌	🍌	🍌			
cherries	🍒							
oranges	🍊	🍊	🍊					
apples	🍎	🍎	🍎	🍎				

Number of children

How many preferred each fruit?

🍇 [3] 🍓 [   ] 🍌 [   ] 🍒 [   ] 🍊 [   ] 🍎 [   ]

Which fruit? Draw.

5 [🍌]   8 [   ]   1 [   ]   3 [   ]

Say and draw.

The fruit
chosen most often is [   ] .

The fruit
chosen least often is [   ] .

More children chose [   ] than [   ] .   My favorite is [   ] .

60

Draw the other half

Finish the pictures.

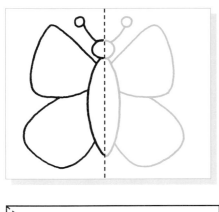

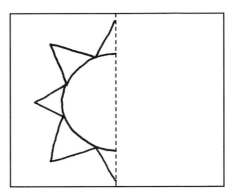

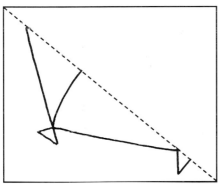
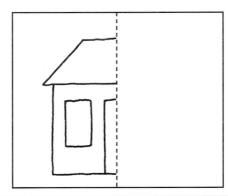
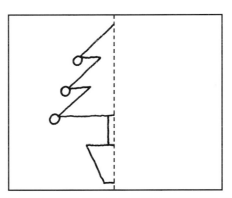

Make the two halves of the pegboards match. Color them in.

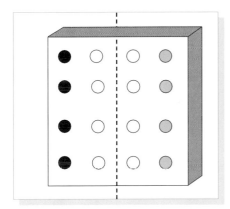
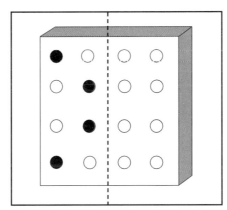
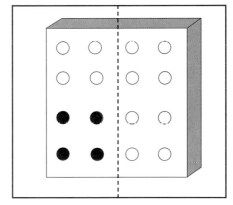

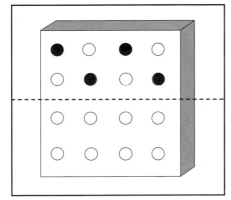
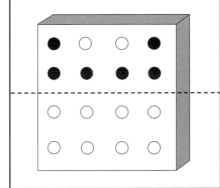
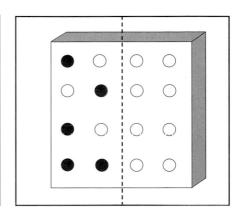

Where's the bear?

on | yes
next to | no

inside |
on top |

inside |
up |

behind |
beside |

on |
in |

in front |
inside |

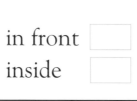

under |
behind |

above |
under |

on | .
over |

down |
up |

Numbers

Write the numbers.

0 0 0 0

1 1 1 1

2 2 2 2

3 3 3 3

4 4 4 4

5 5 5 5

6 6 6 6

7 7 7 7

8 8 8 8

9 9 9 9

Continue the pattern.

1 5 7   1 5 7

3 6 9   3 6 9

2 4 8   2 4 8

Numbers

Which numbers are the snakes hiding?
Say the numbers as you write the answers.

1	2	3	4	5	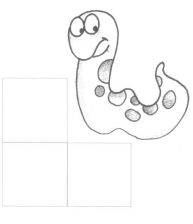	7	8	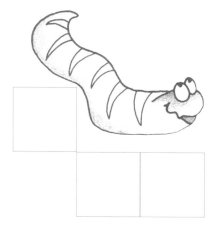
11			14	15		17		19	20
21	22		24	25		27	28		30
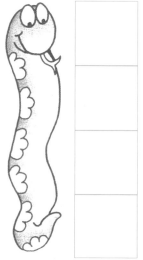	32	33	34	35		37	38	
41			44	45	46			49	50

| 9 | 10 |

Addition

How many are there in all? Color them in.

△ △ △ + △ △ △ = ▲ ▲ ▲ ▲ ▲ ▲ △ △

◯◯◯ + ◯◯◯ = ◯◯◯◯◯◯◯◯◯◯◯
◯◯◯

□ □ + □ □ = □ □ □ □ □ □ □ □

☾ ☾ + ☾ ☾ ☾ = ☾ ☾ ☾
☾ ☾ ☾ ☾ ☾ ☾ ☾
☾ ☾

🐟🐟🐟 + 🐟 = 🐟🐟🐟
🐟🐟🐟 🐟 🐟🐟🐟
🐟🐟 🐟🐟🐟
🐟 🐟🐟🐟

1 less or 1 more

Count, draw, and write.

1 less · 1 less · **56** · 1 more · 1 more

1 less · **61** · 1 more

1 less · **79** · 1 more

1 less · **98** · 1 more

1 less · **17** · 1 more

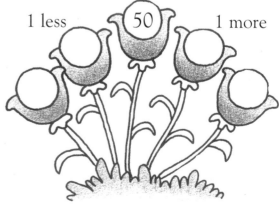

1 less · **50** · 1 more

Tallies

Which tally marks show 13?

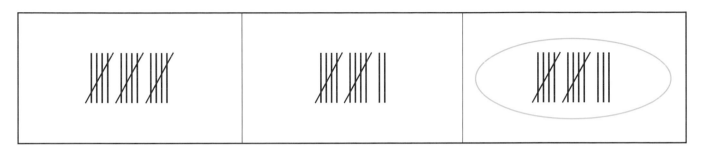

Which tally marks show 15?

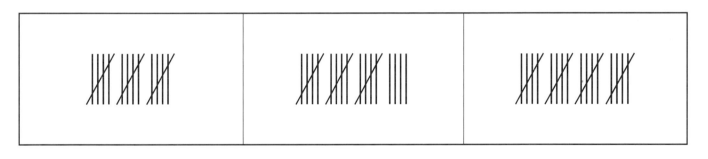

Which tally marks show 17?

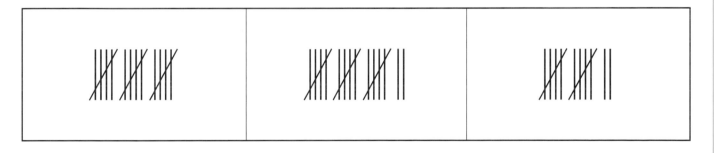

Which tally marks show 23?

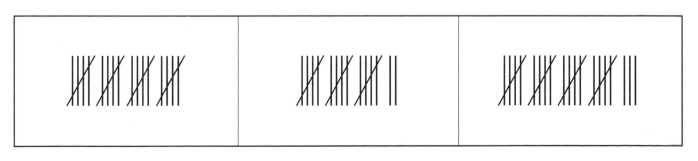

Using a table

Use the table to answer the questions.
Circle the correct answer.

Glasses of water

Name	Saturday	Sunday
Sasha	4	6
William	6	4
Anita	6	8
Nabi	5	7

Who drank less water on Saturday?   (Sasha)   Nabi

How many glasses of water did Anita drink
on Sunday?   4   8   7

Who drank 7 glasses of water on Sunday?   Nabi   Anita

Who drank a total of 10 glasses of water?   Nabi   William

Who drank the most glasses of water?   Nabi   Anita

Who drank less water on Sunday?   Anita   Nabi

How many glasses of water did Sasha and
William together drink on Saturday?   10   12

Patterns of 2, 5, and 10

Count, color, and find a pattern.

Count by 2s and color them green.

1	2	3	4	5	6	7	8	9	10
11	12	13	14	15	16	17	18	19	20
21	22	23	24	25	26	27	28	29	30
31	32	33	34	35	36	37	38	39	40
41	42	43	44	45	46	47	48	49	50

Count by 5s and color them purple.

1	2	3	4	5	6	7	8	9	10
11	12	13	14	15	16	17	18	19	20
21	22	23	24	25	26	27	28	29	30
31	32	33	34	35	36	37	38	39	40
41	42	43	44	45	46	47	48	49	50

Count by 10s and color them yellow.

1	2	3	4	5	6	7	8	9	10
11	12	13	14	15	16	17	18	19	20
21	22	23	24	25	26	27	28	29	30
31	32	33	34	35	36	37	38	39	40
41	42	43	44	45	46	47	48	49	50

More or less

Connect the spaceships to the planets and the rockets to the stars.

1 more

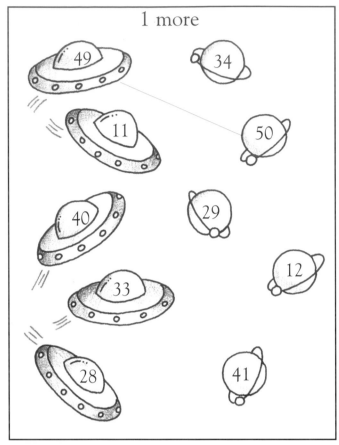

10 more

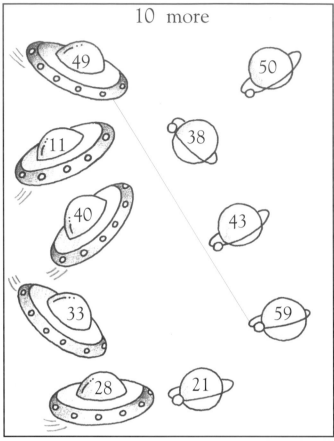

1 less

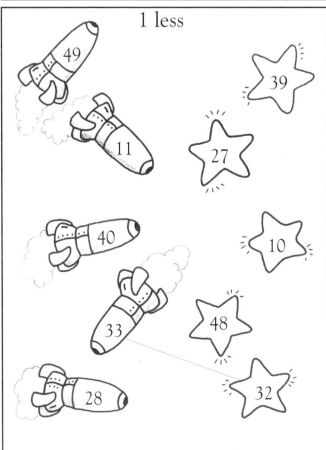

10 less

Ordering

Write the numbers in order.

smallest first

| 7 | 16 | 26 | | | |

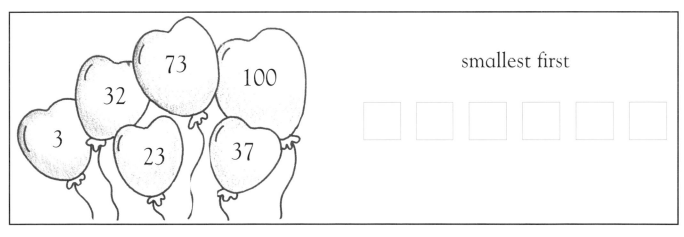

greatest first

| | | | | | |

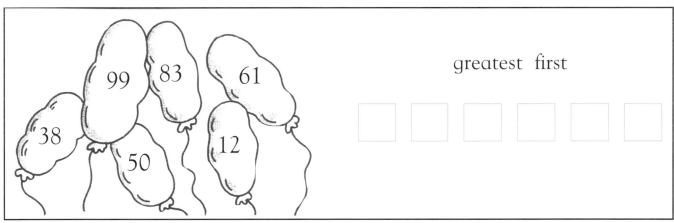

smallest first

| | | | | | |

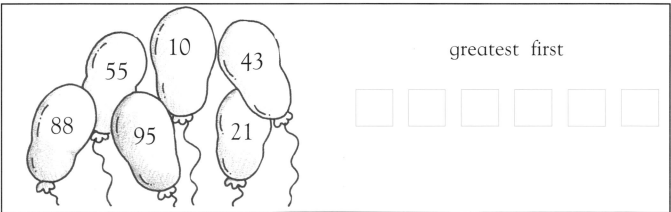

greatest first

| | | | | | |

Fractions of shapes

Color one third ($\frac{1}{3}$).

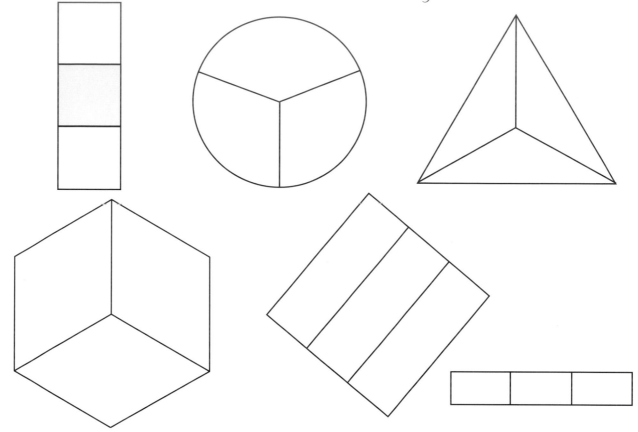

Is it $\frac{1}{3}$? Yes or no.

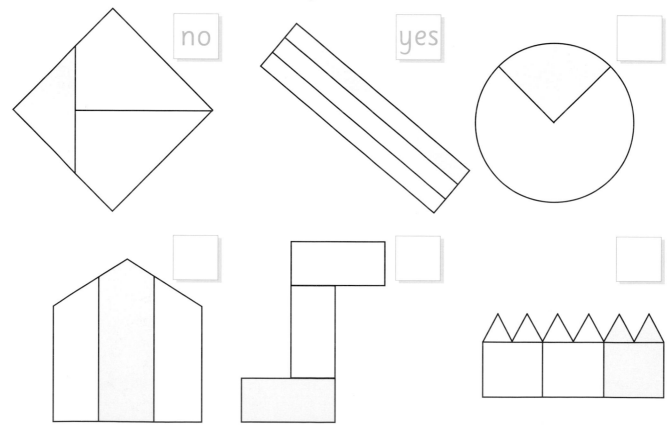

no   yes

Addition

How many are there in all? Color them in.

○○○ + ○○○○○ = ●●●●●●●○

○○○○ + ○○○ = ○○○○○○○○○○○○

Adding coins

Use three coins each time.
How many different totals can you make?

10¢ + 1¢ + 1¢ = 12¢

25¢ + 5¢ + 1¢ = 31¢

Addition grid

Draw rings around the pairs of numbers that add up to 20.

15	5	3	10	10	4	19
8	6	20	0	9	1	10
12	13	7	12	0	16	1
4	5	10	16	4	5	10
9	2	18	7	20	3	10
11	3	3	1	0	11	9
17	1	1	19	3	18	11

Doubles

Write the missing numbers.

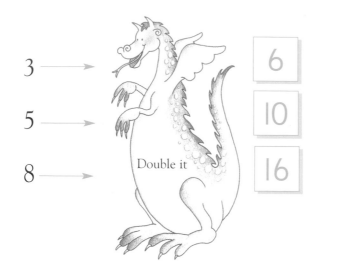

3 →
5 →
8 →

Double it

6
10
16

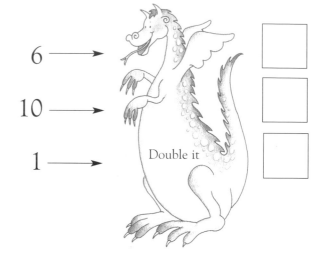

6 →
10 →
1 →

Double it

☐
☐
☐

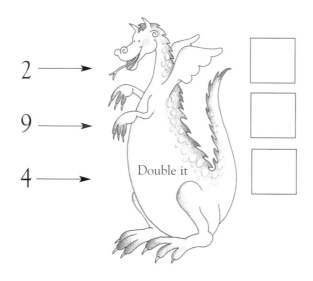

2 →
9 →
4 →

Double it

☐
☐
☐

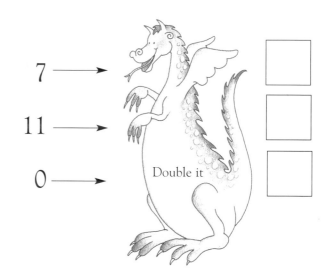

7 →
11 →
0 →

Double it

☐
☐
☐

What has been doubled? Write the missing number.

Double 4 is 8

Double 8 is 16

Double ☐ is 18

Double ☐ is 20

Double ☐ is 14

Double ☐ is 6

Double ☐ is 12

Double ☐ is 10

Double ☐ is 4

Double ☐ is 2

Fact families

Complete each fact family.

4,   5,   9

4	+	5	=	9
5	+	4	=	9
9	−	4	=	5
9	−	5	=	4

3,   4,   7

3	+	4	=	7
4	+	3	=	
7	−	3	=	4
7	−	4	=	

2,   4,   6

2	+	4	=	6
4	+	2	=	
6	−	4	=	2
6	−	2	=	

3,   5,   8

3	+	5	=	8
5	+	3	=	
8	−	3	=	5
8	−	5	=	

Addition

Add to find each sum.

```
  2 3
+   4
─────
  27
```

Add to find each sum.

```
  1 8        2 3        3 2        2 0
+   1      +   4      +   6      +   5
─────      ─────      ─────      ─────
```

```
  3 0        5 0        1 0        4 0
+   9      +   3      +   4      +   2
─────      ─────      ─────      ─────
```

```
  4 2        1 6        3 4        5 2
+   3      +   3      +   3      +   5
─────      ─────      ─────      ─────
```

```
  2 7        1 2        2 0        1 1
+   1      +   4      +   7      +   7
─────      ─────      ─────      ─────
```

Subtraction

Subtract to find the difference.

```
   24
 −  3
   21
```

Subtract to find each difference.

```
   18        25        36        25
 −  1      −  2      −  2      −  4
 ____      ____      ____      ____
```

```
   39        53        14        49
 −  7      −  2      −  4      −  3
 ____      ____      ____      ____
```

```
   46        16        38        57
 −  3      −  5      −  7      −  5
 ____      ____      ____      ____
```

```
   27        14        27        17
 −  1      −  2      −  4      −  1
 ____      ____      ____      ____
```

Subtraction

Subtract to find the difference.

$$\begin{array}{r} 80 \\ -30 \\ \hline 50 \end{array}$$

Subtract to find each difference.

$$\begin{array}{r} 30 \\ -20 \\ \hline \end{array}$$
$$\begin{array}{r} 50 \\ -30 \\ \hline \end{array}$$
$$\begin{array}{r} 40 \\ -20 \\ \hline \end{array}$$
$$\begin{array}{r} 20 \\ -10 \\ \hline \end{array}$$

$$\begin{array}{r} 40 \\ -30 \\ \hline \end{array}$$
$$\begin{array}{r} 50 \\ -20 \\ \hline \end{array}$$
$$\begin{array}{r} 60 \\ -40 \\ \hline \end{array}$$
$$\begin{array}{r} 90 \\ -30 \\ \hline \end{array}$$

$$\begin{array}{r} 70 \\ -30 \\ \hline \end{array}$$
$$\begin{array}{r} 90 \\ -40 \\ \hline \end{array}$$
$$\begin{array}{r} 40 \\ -10 \\ \hline \end{array}$$
$$\begin{array}{r} 50 \\ -40 \\ \hline \end{array}$$

$$\begin{array}{r} 90 \\ -70 \\ \hline \end{array}$$
$$\begin{array}{r} 80 \\ -10 \\ \hline \end{array}$$
$$\begin{array}{r} 60 \\ -50 \\ \hline \end{array}$$
$$\begin{array}{r} 40 \\ -40 \\ \hline \end{array}$$

Subtraction

Subtract to find the difference.

```
  8 7
- 3 4
─────
  53
```

Subtract to find each difference.

```
  3 9          5 8          4 4          2 7
- 2 7        - 3 2        - 1 1        - 1 7
─────        ─────        ─────        ─────


  4 6          5 9          7 5          8 8
- 3 3        - 4 6        - 3 1        - 1 4
─────        ─────        ─────        ─────


  7 7          9 3          6 7          3 8
- 3 3        - 2 2        - 5 3        - 2 2
─────        ─────        ─────        ─────


  9 9          8 2          6 9          4 7
- 7 9        - 7 0        - 6 9        - 4 6
─────        ─────        ─────        ─────
```

Real-life problems

All the piggy banks need 30¢. Draw different coins in each one.
You can use any coin more than once.

Real-life problems

| 6¢ | 5¢ | 4¢ | 2¢ | 1¢ |

Draw the stamps on the letters.
You can use any stamp more than once.

Ms. Heather Hedgehog
1 The Leaf Pile
Snowdrop Corner
Garden City

12¢

Doctor Dilly Dinosaur
6 The Swamp
Mud Town

20¢

Rachel Robot
999 Mechanical Mansion
Metalville

24¢

Cheeky Charlie Chimp
100 Banana Court
Giggleton
Apeland

18¢

Mr. Bertie Bear
The Toy Box
Betty's Bedroom
The Big House

11¢

Samuel Spider
Wonder Web
Grandpa's Greenhouse
South Central Garden

25¢

Subtraction tables

Finish each table.

−	2	3	5	10
11	9	8		
15	13			
20				

−	1	6	8	9
14				
19	18	13	11	
25				

−	0	4	7	11
12			5	
28			21	
30				

Counting down

The rocket can only lift off at zero.
Use subtraction to get to 0 in 4 moves.

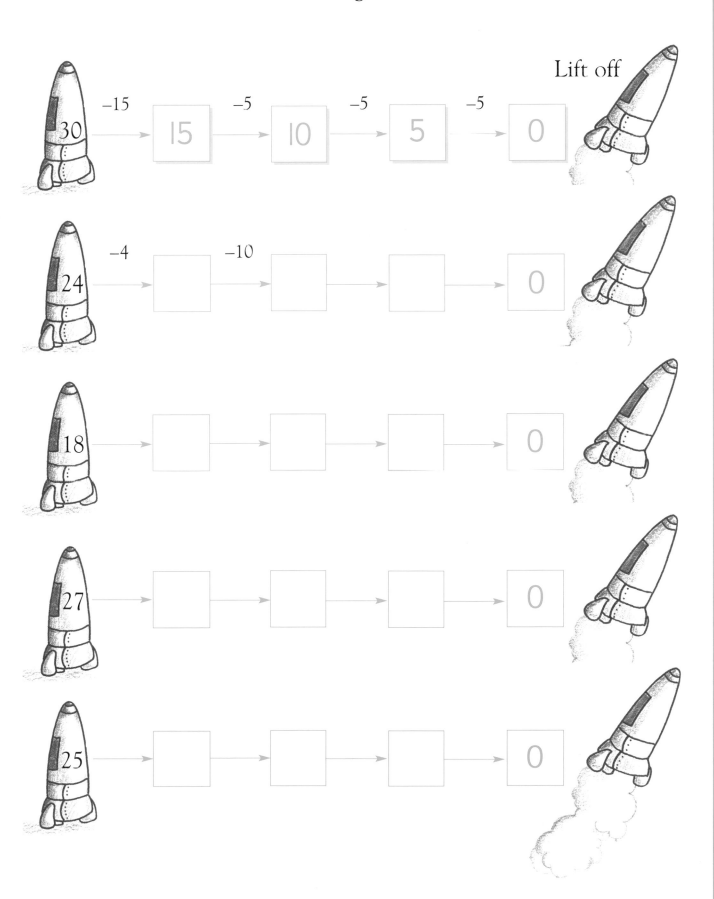

−15 → 15 −5 → 10 −5 → 5 −5 → 0   Lift off

−4 → [ ] −10 → [ ] → [ ] → 0

24

18 → [ ] → [ ] → [ ] → 0

27 → [ ] → [ ] → [ ] → 0

25 → [ ] → [ ] → [ ] → 0

Clocks

Write the times under the clocks.

4 o'clock

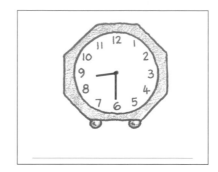

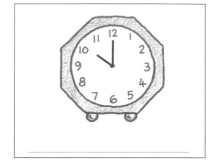

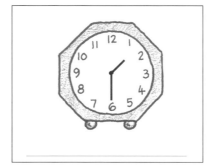

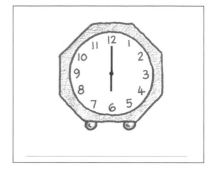

Draw the hands.

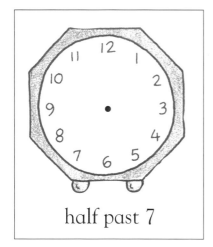

half past 7

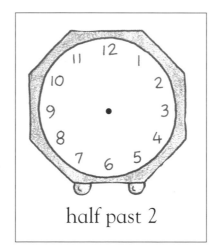

half past 2

10 o'clock

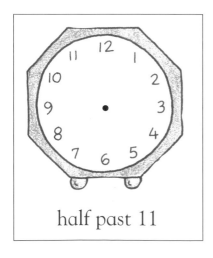

half past 11

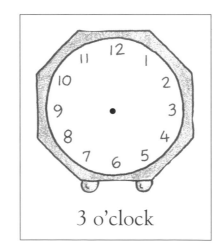

3 o'clock

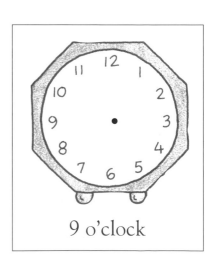

9 o'clock

Digital clocks

Write the times under the clocks.

half past 12 _____ _____

_____ _____ _____

Fill in the digital times on the clock faces.

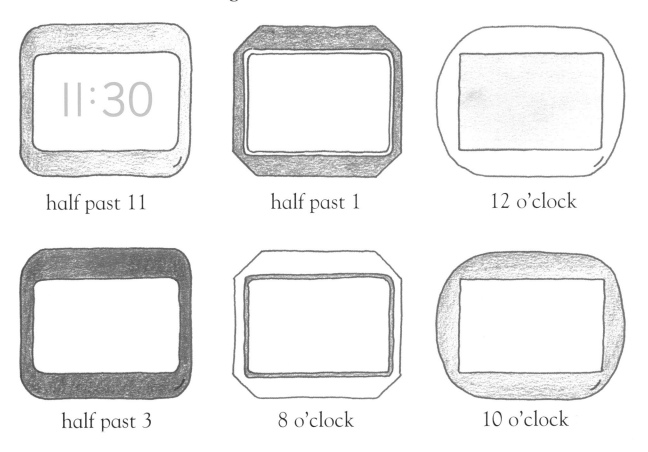

half past 11   half past 1   12 o'clock

half past 3   8 o'clock   10 o'clock

Match the times

Draw a line to connect the matching times.

half past nine

half past 9

2 o'clock

6 o'clock

six o'clock

2 o'clock

half past six

9 o'clock

half past twelve

half past 6

nine o'clock

half past 12

Do you know?

Put the months in order by writing a number on each page.

How many ...

... seconds in a minute? ☐ ... minutes in an hour? ☐

... hours in a day? ☐ ... days in a week? ☐

... days in a year? ☐ ... months in a year? ☐

Learn this rhyme.

30 days have September,
April, June, and November.

All the rest have 31,
Except February alone
That has 28 days clear
29 in each leap year.

How many days are there in your birthday month? ☐

Congruent shapes

Ring the shape that matches the first shape.

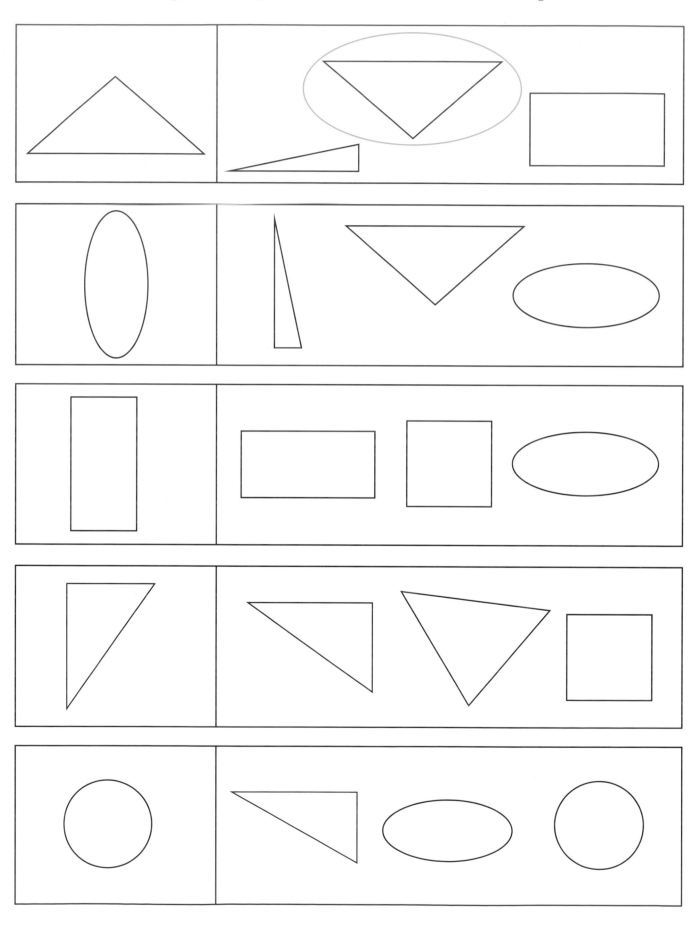

Venn diagrams

Flowers with green petals

Flowers with white petals

How many flowers have ...

 ... green petals? `7` ... white petals? `10` ... both green and white petals? `2`

Shapes with straight sides

Shapes with curved sides

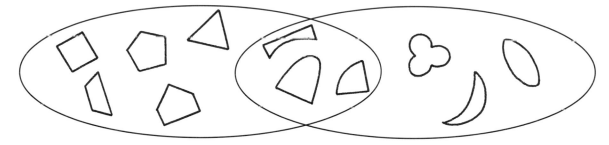

How many shapes have ...

 ... straight sides? ☐ ... curved sides? ☐ ... straight and curved sides? ☐

Odd numbers

Numbers greater than ten

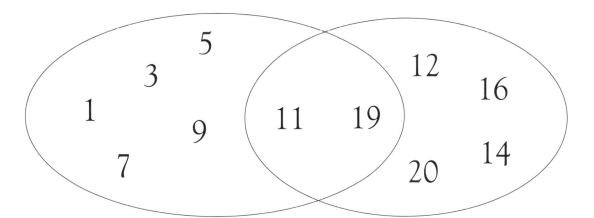

How many numbers are ...

 ... odd? ☐ ... more than ten? ☐ ... odd and more than ten? ☐

Similar shapes

Ring the shape that is the same but a different size.

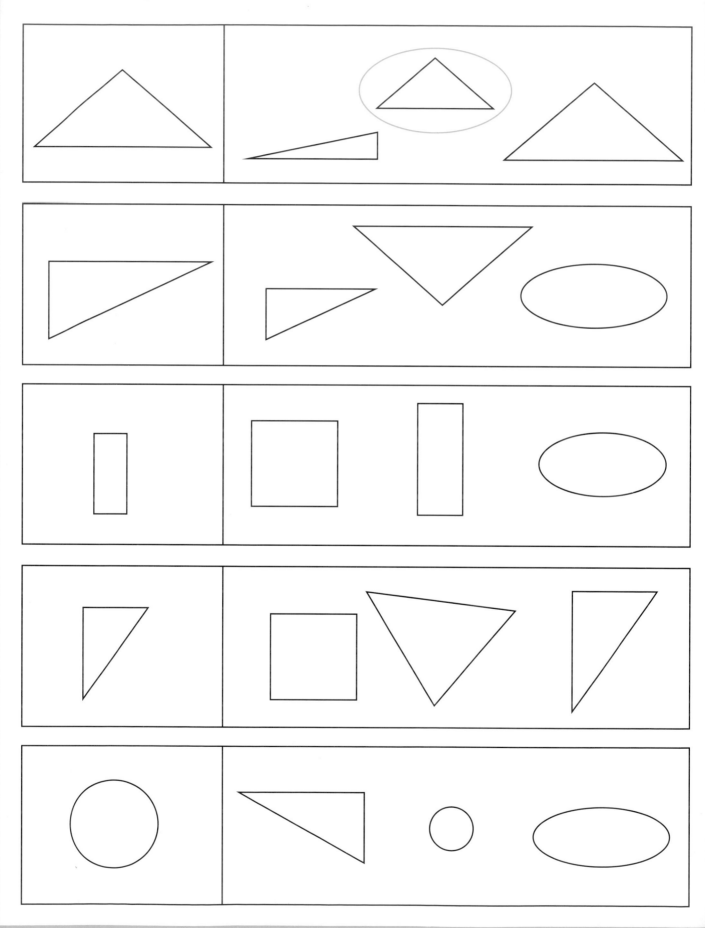

2-dimensional shapes

Add the costs to find the cost of each picture.

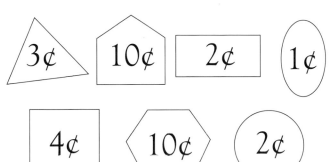

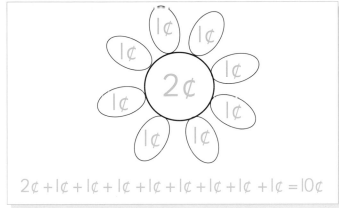

2¢ + 1¢ + 1¢ + 1¢ + 1¢ + 1¢ + 1¢ + 1¢ + 1¢ = 10¢

House

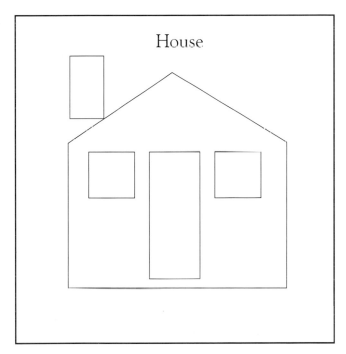

Bee and honeycomb

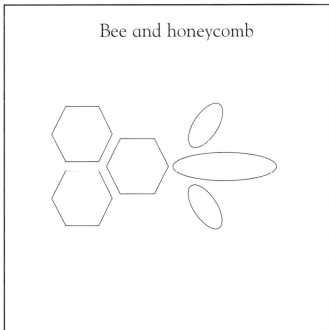

Teddy bear

Crown

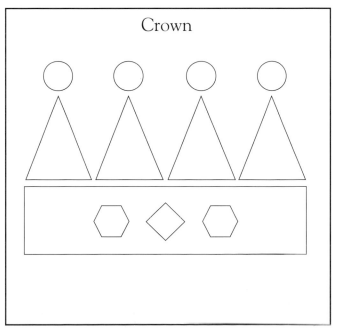

3-dimensional shapes

Label the 3-D shapes.
(cone, cylinder, pyramid, cube, sphere, rectangular prism)

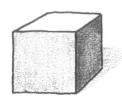  

cube _____ _____ _____ _____

 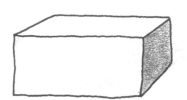

_____ _____

How many of each 3-D shape?

cube	3	rectangular prism		cone		cylinder	

pyramid		sphere	

Read, write, and draw

Write the numbers and draw the pictures.

76   seventy-six

59   _____

_____   forty-five

112   one hundred twelve

_____   _____

107   one hundred seven

_____   one hundred fifty

Counting

Count on forward or backward by 10s.
Write the missing numbers.

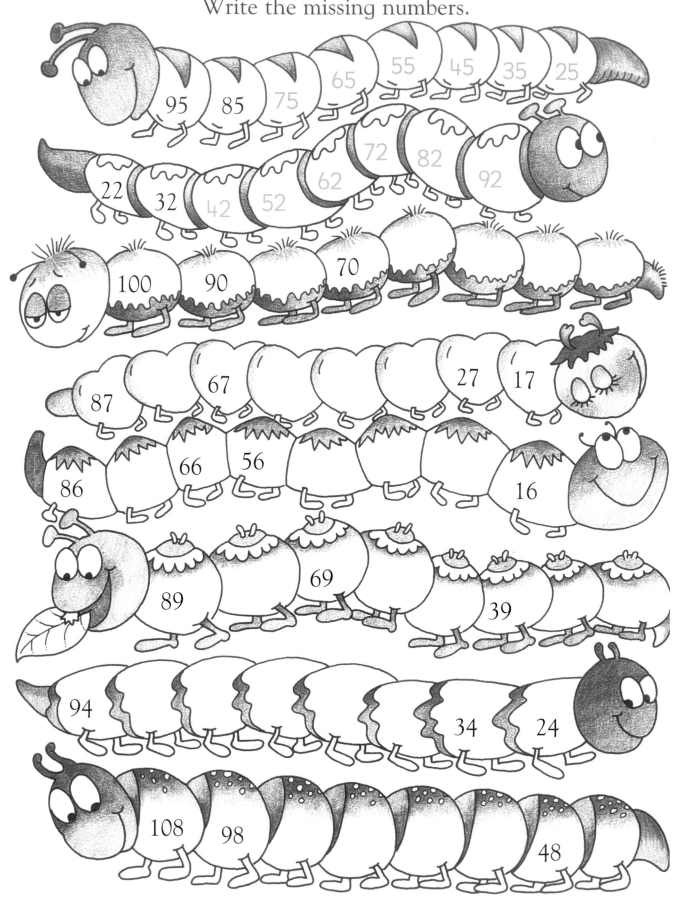

Bar graphs

Fruit

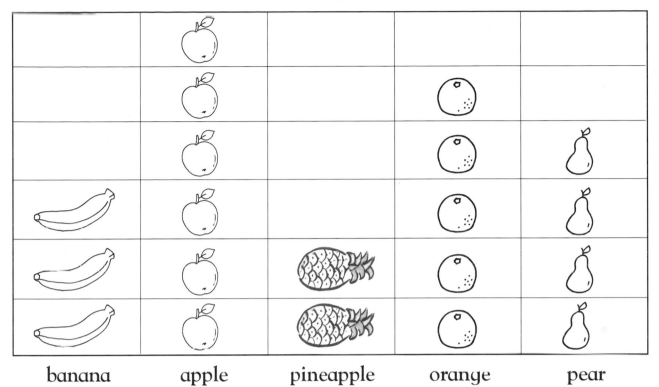

| banana | apple | pineapple | orange | pear |

How many pears are there? 4   How many bananas are there?

The graph shows 6   .   The graph shows 2   .

How many more oranges are there than bananas?

How many apples and pears are there altogether?

Ellen's marbles

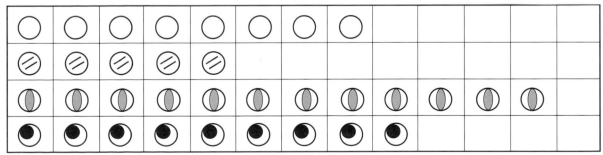

How many ⊘ does Ellen have?   How many ◗ does Ellen have?

How many fewer ● than ◗ does she have?

How many ○ and ⊘ does she have altogether?

Subtraction

If each child eats 1 slice,
how many slices will be left?   5

If the children eat 6 slices,
how many slices will be left?   2

If the children eat 8 slices,
how many slices will be left?

If each child reads 1 book,
how many books will be left?

How many books will be left if the
children take 6 books altogether?

How many books will be left
if the children take 9 books?

If the dog buries 1 ball,
how many balls are left?

Write a subtraction sentence.   7 − 1 = 6

If the dog buries 3 balls,
how many balls are left?

Write a subtraction sentence.

2s, 5s, and 10s

Count by 2s, 5s, and 10s to help you connect the dots.

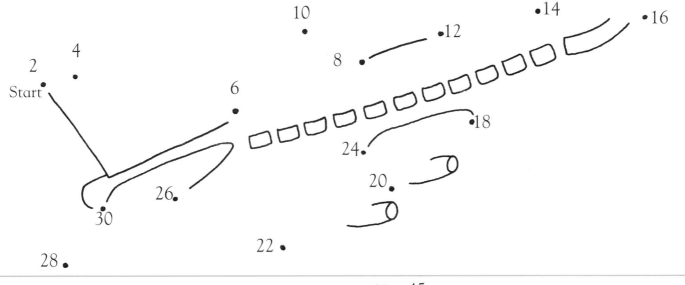

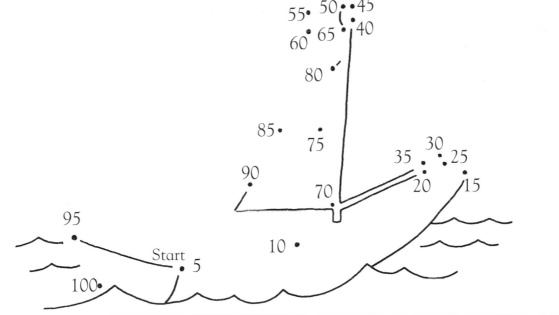

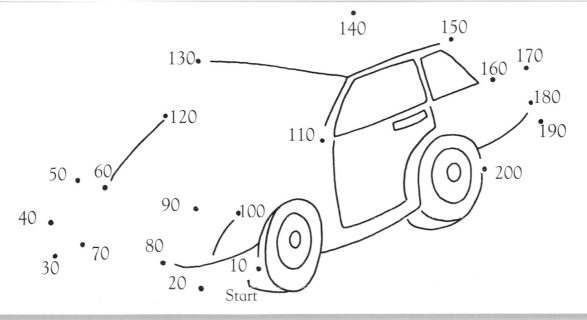

Comparing

Complete the boxes.

2 less	number	2 more
51	53	55

number	between	number
96	97 98	99

number	between	number
20		24

3 less	number	3 more
	30	

2 less	number	2 more
	29	

number	between	number
18		22

number	between	number
131		134

10 less	number	10 more
	119	

5 less	number	5 more
	85	

number	between	number
40		45

number	between	number
99		102

5 less	number	5 more
	156	

Ordering

Find the totals.

11¢

Write the totals in order, greatest first.

| 1st | 2nd | 3rd 11¢ | 4th | 5th |

Find the totals.

40¢

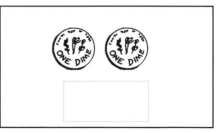

Write the totals in order, smallest first.

| 1st | 2nd | 3rd | 4th | 5th 40¢ |

Subtraction

How many fewer apples
are on the left tree than on the right tree?

Write the subtraction sentence.

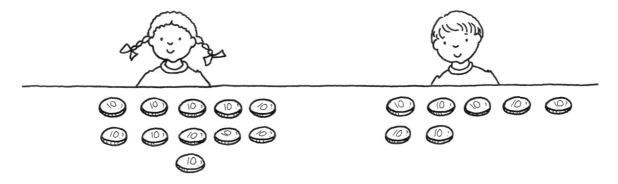

How many more dimes does Tasha have than Juan?

What is the subtraction sentence?

How many fewer bricks are
in the left stack than in the right stack?

What is the subtraction sentence?

Matching fractions

Color all the matching squares.

Use yellow for halves.
Use orange for thirds.
Use green for fourths.

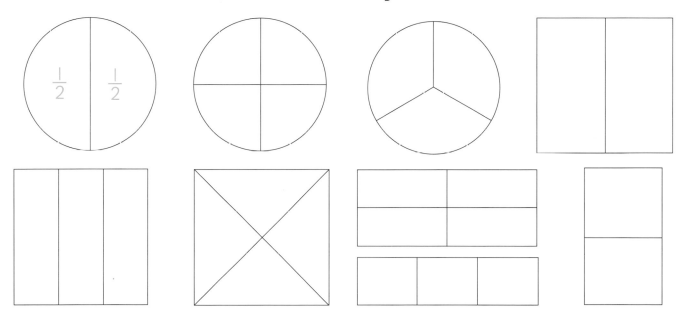

Label each part.

How many thirds in
a whole?

How many fourths in
a whole?

How many halves in
a whole?

How many fourths
in a half?

Money

You have only 3 coins in each purse. Draw the 3 coins that make the exact amount needed. You may use each coin more than once.

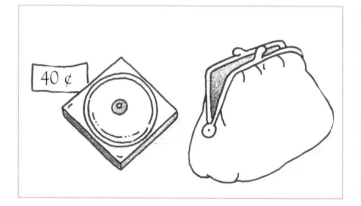

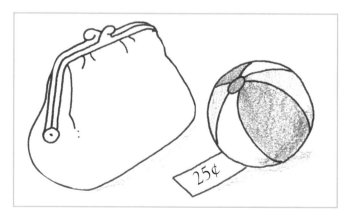

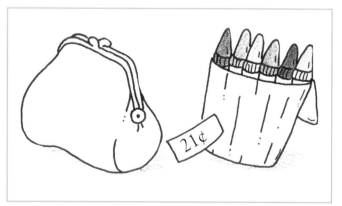

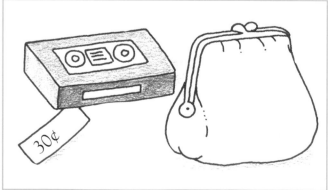

Fact families

Use the 3 numbers to write 4 different facts.

6 + 7 = 13	7 + 6 = 13	13 − 7 = 6	13 − 6 = 7
16 + 4 = 20	+ =	− =	− =
6 + 5 = 11			
7 + 8 = 15			
8 + 12 = 20			
10 + 8 = 18			
8 + 9 = 17			
9 + 7 = 16			
14 + 6 = 20			
11 + 8 = 19			

Adding money

Add the money. Write the totals in the right squares.

+	2¢	5¢	8¢	6¢
3¢				9¢
11¢				
29¢		34¢		
32¢				

+	2¢	4¢	6¢	9¢	3¢
17¢					
20¢				29¢	
33¢	35¢				
41¢					

Using doubles

Use the doubles to find the answers.

6 + 6 = 12	10 + 10 = 20
6 + 7 6 + 6 + 1 = 13	10 + 11 10 + 10 + 1 = 21
6 + 5 6 + 6 − 1 = 11	10 + 9 10 + 10 − 1 = 19

Use doubles to find the answers.

4 + 4 = ☐   4 + 5 = ☐ + ☐ + 1 = ☐

4 + 3 = ☐ + ☐ − 1 = ☐

7 + 7 = ☐   7 + 8 = ☐ + ☐ + 1 = ☐

7 + 6 = ☐ + ☐ − 1 = ☐

8 + 8 = ☐   8 + 9 = ☐ + ☐ + 1 = ☐

8 + 7 = ☐ + ☐ − 1 = ☐

Double your doubles.

1	double it	2	double it	4		4	double it	☐	double it	☐
2	double it	☐	double it	☐		5	double it	☐	double it	☐
3	double it	☐	double it	☐		6	double it	☐	double it	☐

Adding up

Add the numbers on the sails. Write the totals on the boats.

Add the numbers. Write the totals.

$3 + 4 + 10 =$ ☐ 17 $9 + 0 + 50 =$ ☐ $2 + 70 + 3 =$ ☐

$5 + 40 + 2 =$ ☐ $20 + 7 + 2 =$ ☐ $4 + 5 + 60 =$ ☐

$30 + 4 + 3 =$ ☐ $1 + 50 + 7 =$ ☐ $80 + 8 + 1 =$ ☐

$$\begin{array}{r} 30 \\ 1 \\ +\ 7 \\ \hline \\ \hline \end{array}$$ $$\begin{array}{r} 10 \\ 2 \\ +\ 5 \\ \hline \\ \hline \end{array}$$ $$\begin{array}{r} 50 \\ 2 \\ +\ 4 \\ \hline \\ \hline \end{array}$$ $$\begin{array}{r} 60 \\ 5 \\ +\ 0 \\ \hline \\ \hline \end{array}$$

Count by 2s

Draw the pictures. Count by 2s. Write the totals.

Sasha has 4 hutches. There are 2 rabbits in each hutch.

8 rabbits

Joel has 3 boxes. There are 2 pencils in each box.

Mrs. Reaves has 6 flower pots. There are 2 flowers in each pot.

Mr. Hastings has 5 fish. Each fish has 2 eyes.

Draw the pictures, then write the answers.

There are 6 birds. There are 2 birds in each tree. How many trees are there?

There are 8 tarts. There are 2 tarts on each plate. How many plates are there?

Addition

Add to find each sum.

```
  42        84        18
+ 13      + 10      + 21
  55        94        39
```

Add to find each sum.

```
  15        68        33        32
+ 34      + 21      + 11      + 43
_____     _____     _____     _____


  54        27        35        11
+ 12      + 21      + 52      + 11
_____     _____     _____     _____


  72        15        10        86
+ 23      + 53      + 19      + 11
_____     _____     _____     _____


  13        36        70        64
+ 42      + 32      + 14      + 25
_____     _____     _____     _____


  21        42        18        16
+ 53      + 41      + 11      + 20
_____     _____     _____     _____
```

Addition

Add to find each sum.

```
    65        14        50
  + 31      + 24      + 10
  ————      ————      ————
    96        38        60
```

Add to find each sum.

```
    24        57        30        17
  + 24      + 11      + 45      + 32
  ————      ————      ————      ————
```

```
    64        15        52        55
  + 22      + 13      + 21      + 40
  ————      ————      ————      ————
```

```
    16        29        61        74
  + 33      + 20      + 35      + 12
  ————      ————      ————      ————
```

Michael has 21 fish. His dad gives him 11 more fish. How many fish does Michael have?

Sonia read 13 books one month. She read 15 books the next month. How many books did she read in all?

Addition and subtraction

Write the missing numbers.

$$? + 8 = 12 \qquad 7 - ? = 1$$
$$4 + 8 = 12 \qquad 7 - 6 = 1$$

Write the missing numbers.

$15 - \underline{} = 10$ $\qquad$ $\underline{} + 3 = 6$ $\qquad$ $8 - \underline{} = 2$

$9 + \underline{} = 11$ $\qquad$ $\underline{} - 8 = 0$ $\qquad$ $\underline{} + 5 = 14$

$\underline{} + 3 = 10$ $\qquad$ $6 - \underline{} = 2$ $\qquad$ $\underline{} - 10 = 7$

$\underline{} - 4 = 1$ $\qquad$ $2 + \underline{} = 7$ $\qquad$ $1 + \underline{} = 4$

$14 - \underline{} = 7$ $\qquad$ $\underline{} + 1 = 9$ $\qquad$ $3 + \underline{} = 12$

$8 + \underline{} = 14$ $\qquad$ $\underline{} - 1 = 2$ $\qquad$ $12 - \underline{} = 6$

$18 - \underline{} = 9$ $\qquad$ $\underline{} + 6 = 11$ $\qquad$ $\underline{} - 1 = 0$

$\underline{} - 7 = 4$ $\qquad$ $4 + \underline{} = 13$ $\qquad$ $\underline{} + 5 = 8$

$\underline{} + 3 = 5$ $\qquad$ $16 - \underline{} = 10$ $\qquad$ $8 + \underline{} = 18$

$5 + \underline{} = 12$ $\qquad$ $\underline{} + 4 = 0$ $\qquad$ $9 - \underline{} = 6$

Real-life problems

Look at the picture. Answer the questions.

What time is it ? ....

Today is Friday. What day was it yesterday? ....

How many cupcakes can each person have? ....

If half of the apples were eaten, how many would be left? ....

If each person had 2 drinks, how many drinks would there be altogether? ....

How many more sandwiches are there than apples? ....

If 13 candies were eaten, how many would be left? ....

Each package contains 2 presents. How many presents are there altogether? ....

What shape are the sandwiches? ....

Is there an odd or an even number of chairs? ....

Real-life problems

Complete the pictures, and then write the answers.

There were 12 biscuits. James ate 3.
How many were left?

9

Share 12 marbles equally among
3 people. How many marbles will
each have?

Susie has ten fish. She is given 11 more
for her birthday. How many fish does she
have altogether?

Joe had 5 boxes. He had 3 pencils in
each box. How many pencils did he
have altogether?

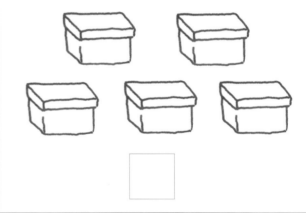

If you share 16 carrots equally among 4
rabbits, how many carrots will each have?

Mom had 16 cups, but she broke 9 of
them. How many cups does she have left?

Addition

Find each sum.

$$\begin{array}{r} 40 \\ +30 \\ \hline 70 \end{array}$$

$$\begin{array}{r} 80 \\ +80 \\ \hline 160 \end{array}$$

$$\begin{array}{r} 20 \\ +50 \\ \hline \end{array}$$

$$\begin{array}{r} 90 \\ +30 \\ \hline \end{array}$$

$$\begin{array}{r} 10 \\ +10 \\ \hline \end{array}$$

$$\begin{array}{r} 70 \\ +50 \\ \hline \end{array}$$

$$\begin{array}{r} 80 \\ +40 \\ \hline \end{array}$$

$$\begin{array}{r} 50 \\ +30 \\ \hline \end{array}$$

$$\begin{array}{r} 60 \\ +80 \\ \hline \end{array}$$

$$\begin{array}{r} 50 \\ +50 \\ \hline \end{array}$$

$$\begin{array}{r} 20 \\ +10 \\ \hline \end{array}$$

$$\begin{array}{r} 30 \\ +20 \\ \hline \end{array}$$

$$\begin{array}{r} 40 \\ +70 \\ \hline \end{array}$$

$$\begin{array}{r} 20 \\ +40 \\ \hline \end{array}$$

$$\begin{array}{r} 90 \\ +40 \\ \hline \end{array}$$

$$\begin{array}{r} 10 \\ +30 \\ \hline \end{array}$$

Find each sum.

$70 + 20 = \quad 90$ $80 + 70 =$ $10 + 40 =$

$60 + 60 =$ $30 + 30 =$ $50 + 100 =$

$20 + 70 =$ $70 + 90 =$ $10 + 20 =$

$90 + 60 =$ $40 + 40 =$ $80 + 10 =$

Clocks and watches

Write the times.

4 o'clock

half past 10

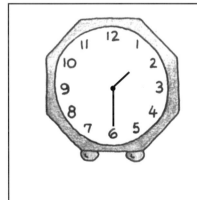

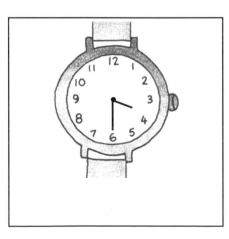

Puzzles

Read the clues and solve the puzzle.

I am a number between 20 and 30. If you
count by fives, you will say my name. Who am I?   25

Read the clues and solve each puzzle.

I am an even number. I am between 6 and 9. Who am I?

7 + 7 is less than I am. 7 + 9 is greater than I am. Who am I?

I am a number less than 10. If you add me to
myself, you will find a number greater than 16. Who am I?

16 – 10 is less than I am. 16 – 8 is greater than I am. Who am I?

I am a number between 7 and 12. If you
count by threes, you will say my name. Who am I?

I am an odd number. I am between 41 and 44. Who am I?

If you subtract me from 14, you will find a
number greater than 11. I am an odd number. Who am I?

If you add me to 50, you will find a number less than 70.
If you count by tens you will say my name. Who am I?

If you add me to 1, you will find
an odd number. I am less than 2. Who am I?

Tables

Water animals

	Has 4 legs	Eats insects	Has a furry coat	Lays eggs
Frog	yes	yes	no	yes
Newt	yes	yes	no	yes
Otter	yes	no	yes	no

Use the table to answer the questions.

What does the frog eat? _insects_

Who lays eggs? _____

Who has a furry coat? _____

Does the otter eat insects? _____

Who has a furry coat and does not lay eggs? _____

School friends

	Age	Hobby	Pet	Favorite color
Dean	7	Computers	Rat	Black
Joe	6	Reading	Rabbit	Purple
Taif	7	Judo	Cat	Orange
Maddie	8	Computers	Parrot	Green

Use the table to answer the questions.

Whose favorite color is black? _Dean's_

Who is the oldest? _____

Who has judo for a hobby? _____

What kind of pet does Joe have? _____

Who likes computers and has a parrot? _____

Who is seven and does not have a rat? _____

Venn diagrams

Things made with metal   Things made with plastic

How many things are ...?

made with plastic? | 6 | made with metal? | 7

made with metal and plastic? | 3 | not made with plastic? | 4

Odd numbers   Numbers greater than 20

3   15
1   21   25   24   26
7   19   30
22

How many numbers are ...?

odd? [ ]   greater than 20? [ ]

odd and greater than 20? [ ]   not odd? [ ]

White things   Green things

How many things are ...?

green? [ ]   white? [ ]

green and white? [ ]   not green? [ ]

Appropriate units of measure

Which unit would you use to measure the
length of each item? Circle the answer.

	(inches)	miles	pounds	quarts
	miles	ounces	pounds	yards

Which unit would you use to measure the
weight of each item? Circle the answer.

	inches	miles	pounds	ounces
	miles	pounds	quarts	ounces

Which unit would you use to measure how much liquid
each container holds? Circle the answer.

	tons	inches	pints	pounds
	miles	inches	ounces	gallons

Symmetry

Draw a line of symmetry on each picture.

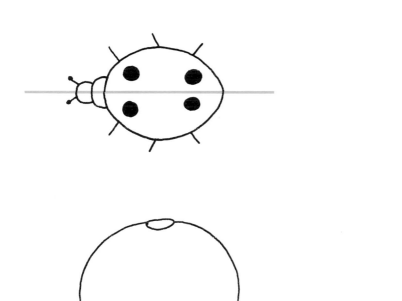

Draw lines of symmetry on these shapes.

2-dimensional shapes

Write the name of the shape. Count the corners and sides.

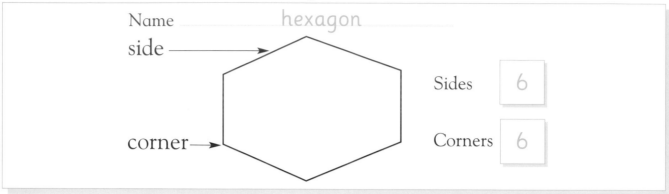

Name   hexagon

side →

corner →

Sides   6

Corners   6

Name

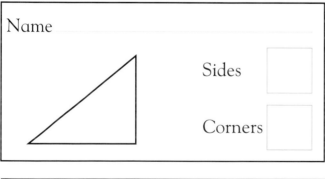

Sides

Corners

Name

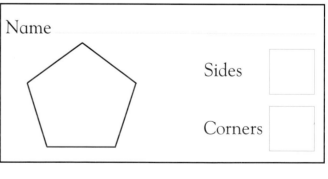

Sides

Corners

Name

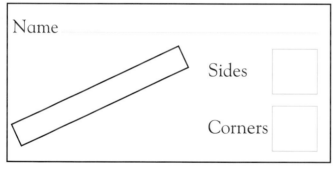

Sides

Corners

Name

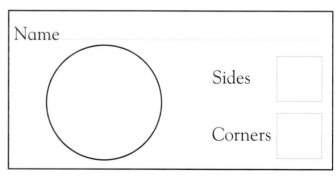

Sides

Corners

Name

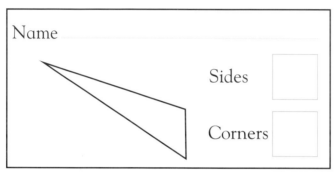

Sides

Corners

Name

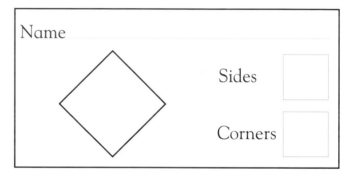

Sides

Corners

Name

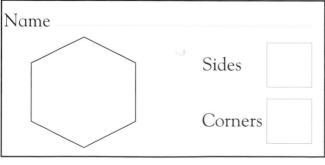

Sides

Corners

Name

Sides

Corners

Equal value

Circle the coins that add up to the amount shown.

7¢	6¢	15¢	8¢	20¢
(5¢)	1¢	1¢	(10¢)	(10¢)
(1¢)	1¢	1¢	5¢	(10¢)
(1¢)	1¢	1¢	1¢	5¢
1¢	1¢	1¢	1¢	1¢
1¢	1¢	5¢	1¢	1¢
1¢	1¢	(10¢)	1¢	1¢

(first column coins 5¢ and two 1¢ circled together)

Write the amounts. Tell if they are equal.

10¢ 5¢
5¢ 5¢ 5¢

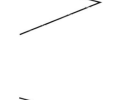

15¢
15¢
equal

10¢ 1¢ 1¢
5¢ 5¢ 1¢ 1¢

1¢ 1¢ 1¢ 1¢ 1¢ 1¢
5¢ 1¢ 1¢

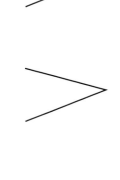

5¢ 5¢
5¢ 1¢ 1¢ 1¢ 1¢

1¢ 5¢ 10¢
5¢ 5¢ 5¢ 1¢

Shapes and places

Look at the shapes and answer the questions.

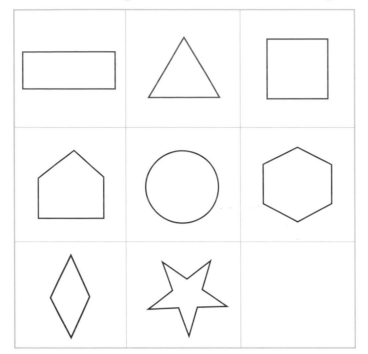

circle

hexagon

diamond

pentagon

rectangle

square

star

triangle

Which shape is ...

underneath the circle?

to the **left** of the triangle?

above the hexagon?

below the pentagon?

between the rectangle and the diamond?

diagonally above the empty space?

beside the diamond?

on top of the diamond?

between the triangle and the star?

on the **right-hand end** of the top row?

in the **center** of the grid?

in the **top left-hand corner**?

Numbers

Which numbers are the snakes hiding?

1	2	3	4	5		7	8	9	
11	12	13		15			18	19	
21	22	23	24		26	27	28		
31			35	36		38	39	40
41		45		47	48	49	50
	52	53	54	55		57	58	59	60
61		63	64	65				69	70
	73	74		76	77	78	79	80
81	82		84				88	
	93		95	96		98		

6

16   17

Counting by 1s, 10s, and 100s

Finish each row.

Count by 1s.	24	25	26	27	28	29
Count by 10s.	31	41	51	61	71	81
Count by 100s.	134	234	334	434	534	634

Finish each row. Count by 1s.

17	18	19		
36	37	38		
69	70	71		
45	46	47		
85	86			91

Finish each row. Count by 10s.

34	44	54		
47	57	67		
78	88	98		
9	19	29		
167	177		197	
305			335	

Finish each row. Count by 100s.

146	246	346		
312	412	512		
508	608	708		
757	857	957		
274	374			974

Counting by 2s

Count by 2s.	12	14	16	18		20		22
Count by 2s.	31	33	35	37		39		41

Finish each row. Count by 2s.

17	19	21					
36	38	40					
72	74	76					
43	45	47					
14	16					26	
39		43					53

Finish each row. Count by 2s.

20							34
75							89
44							58
69							83
31							45
88							102

Finish each row. Count by 2s.

				28			34
			53			59	
					87		91
	48		52				
					97	99	
		50			56		

127

Odd and even

Numbers ending in   0   2   4   6   8   are called even numbers.

Numbers ending in   1   3   5   7   9   are called odd numbers.

Circle the numbers that are even.

10   25   13   34

21   22

18   9   17

6

Circle the numbers that are odd.

90

89   48   56

61   72

63   75   94   77

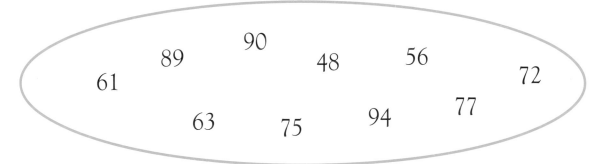

Write the odd numbers between 30 and 50.

Write the even numbers between 71 and 91.

More and less

Which number is 1 more than 49?   50

Which number is 10 less than 764?   754

Which number is 100 less than 187?   87

Write the number that is 1 more than each of these.

| 35 | 78 | 69 | 53 | 9 | 654 |

| 41 | 124 | 167 | 40 | 236 | 473 |

Write the number that is 1 less than each of these.

| 52 | 18 | 20 | 76 | 37 | 150 |

| 50 | 154 | 423 | 100 | 531 | 483 |

Write the number that is 10 more than each of these.

| 46 | 21 | 86 | 153 | 216 |

| 185 | 298 | 399 | 538 | 490 |

| 601 | 990 | 590 | 323 | 480 |

Write the number that is 10 less than each of these.

| 56 | 75 | 86 | 185 | 230 |

| 680 | 451 | 503 | 407 | 805 |

| 600 | 902 | 605 | 702 | 908 |

Write the number that is 100 more than each of these.

| 365 | 76 |

| 960 | 601 |

Write the number that is 100 less than each of these.

| 502 | 100 |

| 809 | 750 |

Fact families

Finish the fact family for each group of numbers.

9

5   4

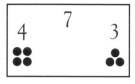

5 + 4 = 9
4 + 5 = 9
9 – 4 = 5
9 – 5 = 4

Finish the fact family for each group of numbers.

7
4   3

4 + 3 =
3 + 4 =
7 – 3 =
7 – 4 =

8
3   5

3 + 5 =
5 + 3 =
8 – 5 =
8 – 3 =

7
6   1

6 + 1 =
1 + 6 =
7 – 1 =
7 – 6 =

6
2   4

2 + 4 =
4 + 2 =
6 – 4 =
6 – 2 =

9
2   7

2 + 7 =
7 + 2 =
9 – 2 =
9 – 7 =

3
2   5

3 + 2 =
2 + 3 =
5 – 2 =
5 – 3 =

3
1   4

3 + 1 =
1 + 3 =
4 – 1 =
4 – 3 =

8
10   2

2 + 8 =
8 + 2 =
10 – 2 =
10 – 8 =

10   5

5 + 5 =
10 – 5 =

4   8

4 + 4 =
8 – 4 =

3   6

3 + 3 =
6 – 3 =

4   2

2 + 2 =
4 – 2 =

Write the fact family for each group of numbers.

3
10   7

9
3   6

8
6   2

7
5   2

130

Fractions

Color one-third ($\frac{1}{3}$) of each shape.

Color one-half ($\frac{1}{2}$) of each shape.

Color one-fourth ($\frac{1}{4}$) of each shape.

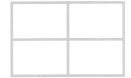

Color one-third ($\frac{1}{3}$) of each shape.

Color one-eighth ($\frac{1}{8}$) of each shape.

Color one-tenth ($\frac{1}{10}$) of each shape.

Adding

Write the answers between the lines.

$$
\begin{array}{r} 35 \\ +16 \\ \hline 51 \end{array}
\qquad
\begin{array}{r} 17 \\ +\ 9 \\ \hline 26 \end{array}
\qquad
\begin{array}{r} 24 \\ +\ 8 \\ \hline 32 \end{array}
$$

Write the answers between the lines.

$$
\begin{array}{r} 24 \\ +\ 9 \\ \hline \end{array}
\qquad
\begin{array}{r} 43 \\ +\ 6 \\ \hline \end{array}
\qquad
\begin{array}{r} 21 \\ +\ 7 \\ \hline \end{array}
\qquad
\begin{array}{r} 46 \\ +\ 5 \\ \hline \end{array}
$$

$$
\begin{array}{r} 43 \\ +\ 7 \\ \hline \end{array}
\qquad
\begin{array}{r} 72 \\ +\ 5 \\ \hline \end{array}
\qquad
\begin{array}{r} 64 \\ +\ 7 \\ \hline \end{array}
\qquad
\begin{array}{r} 38 \\ +\ 8 \\ \hline \end{array}
$$

$$
\begin{array}{r} 46 \\ +10 \\ \hline \end{array}
\qquad
\begin{array}{r} 37 \\ +11 \\ \hline \end{array}
\qquad
\begin{array}{r} 53 \\ +12 \\ \hline \end{array}
\qquad
\begin{array}{r} 49 \\ +\ 9 \\ \hline \end{array}
$$

Write the answers between the lines.

$$
\begin{array}{r} 9 \\ 7 \\ +\ 9 \\ \hline \end{array}
\qquad
\begin{array}{r} 8 \\ 9 \\ +\ 7 \\ \hline \end{array}
\qquad
\begin{array}{r} 7 \\ 9 \\ +\ 6 \\ \hline \end{array}
\qquad
\begin{array}{r} 8 \\ 8 \\ +\ 9 \\ \hline \end{array}
$$

$$
\begin{array}{r} 12¢ \\ 6¢ \\ +10¢ \\ \hline \end{array}
\qquad
\begin{array}{r} 18¢ \\ 7¢ \\ +10¢ \\ \hline \end{array}
\qquad
\begin{array}{r} 8¢ \\ 11¢ \\ +\ 6¢ \\ \hline \end{array}
\qquad
\begin{array}{r} 13¢ \\ 9¢ \\ +\ 6¢ \\ \hline \end{array}
$$

$$
\begin{array}{r} 20¢ \\ 7¢ \\ +10¢ \\ \hline \end{array}
\qquad
\begin{array}{r} 15¢ \\ 10¢ \\ +\ 2¢ \\ \hline \end{array}
\qquad
\begin{array}{r} 8¢ \\ 10¢ \\ +\ 4¢ \\ \hline \end{array}
\qquad
\begin{array}{r} 10¢ \\ 8¢ \\ +10¢ \\ \hline \end{array}
$$

Estimating length

Circle the longest string.

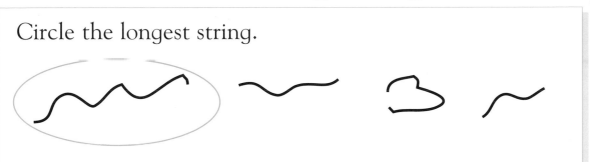

Circle the shortest string.

Circle the longest string.

Look at the ruler. Circle the closest measure.

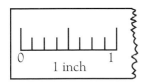

0   1 inch   1

1 inch   2 inches   3 inches   4 inches

2 inches   3 inches   4 inches   6 inches

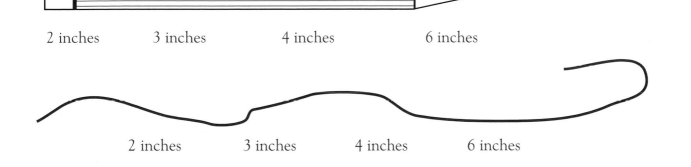

2 inches   3 inches   4 inches   6 inches

Subtracting

Write the answers between the lines.

$$
\begin{array}{r} 28 \\ -\ 16 \\ \hline 12 \end{array}
\qquad
\begin{array}{r} {\scriptstyle 2\ 11} \\ \cancel{31} \\ -\ 14 \\ \hline 17 \end{array}
\qquad
\begin{array}{r} {\scriptstyle 3\ 10} \\ \cancel{40} \\ -\ 17 \\ \hline 23 \end{array}
$$

Write the answers between the lines.

$$
\begin{array}{r} 27 \\ -\ 14 \\ \hline \end{array}
\qquad
\begin{array}{r} 41 \\ -\ 25 \\ \hline \end{array}
\qquad
\begin{array}{r} 60 \\ -\ 37 \\ \hline \end{array}
\qquad
\begin{array}{r} 53 \\ -\ 38 \\ \hline \end{array}
$$

$$
\begin{array}{r} 32 \\ -\ 14 \\ \hline \end{array}
\qquad
\begin{array}{r} 45 \\ -\ 26 \\ \hline \end{array}
\qquad
\begin{array}{r} 33 \\ -\ 20 \\ \hline \end{array}
\qquad
\begin{array}{r} 50 \\ -\ 27 \\ \hline \end{array}
$$

$$
\begin{array}{r} 47 \\ -\ 28 \\ \hline \end{array}
\qquad
\begin{array}{r} 25 \\ -\ \ 6 \\ \hline \end{array}
\qquad
\begin{array}{r} 63 \\ -\ 44 \\ \hline \end{array}
\qquad
\begin{array}{r} 36 \\ -\ 28 \\ \hline \end{array}
$$

$$
\begin{array}{r} 28¢ \\ -\ 16¢ \\ \hline \end{array}
\qquad
\begin{array}{r} 43¢ \\ -\ 35¢ \\ \hline \end{array}
\qquad
\begin{array}{r} 50¢ \\ -\ 26¢ \\ \hline \end{array}
\qquad
\begin{array}{r} 48¢ \\ -\ 37¢ \\ \hline \end{array}
$$

$$
\begin{array}{r} 53¢ \\ -\ 35¢ \\ \hline \end{array}
\qquad
\begin{array}{r} 37¢ \\ -\ 28¢ \\ \hline \end{array}
\qquad
\begin{array}{r} 70¢ \\ -\ 47¢ \\ \hline \end{array}
\qquad
\begin{array}{r} 45¢ \\ -\ 38¢ \\ \hline \end{array}
$$

$$
\begin{array}{r} 40¢ \\ -\ \ 8¢ \\ \hline \end{array}
\qquad
\begin{array}{r} 60¢ \\ -\ 26¢ \\ \hline \end{array}
\qquad
\begin{array}{r} 41¢ \\ -\ 14¢ \\ \hline \end{array}
\qquad
\begin{array}{r} 54¢ \\ -\ 36¢ \\ \hline \end{array}
$$

Simple tally charts and bar graphs

Look at the tally chart and then answer the question.

blue	|||| |||| |||| |||
red	|||| ||

How many votes did blue receive? 18

Look at the tally chart and then answer the questions.

Favorite ice cream flavors

vanilla	|||| ||||	
chocolate	|||| |||| |||| |||| ||||
strawberry	|||| |||| |||| |||

Which flavor had the most votes?

Which flavor had 11 votes?

What was the difference in votes between the most popular flavor and strawberry?

Look at the bar graph and then answer the questions.

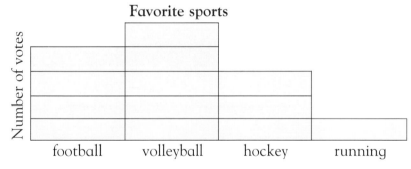

Favorite sports

Which sport did four children vote for?

How many votes did volleyball receive?

Which was the least popular sport?

How many children voted altogether?

How many more voted for football than for hockey?

Addition properties

Circle the number that makes the sentence true.

___ + 3 = 3   15 + ___ = 15

0   3   6   30   0   5

___ + 23 = 23 + 16   25 + 41 = 41 + ___

16   23   46   16   66   25

___ + 45 = 45   70 + 0 = 0 + ___

45   0   1   70   0   700

Complete the number sentences.

   + 27 = 27   90 + 0 =   13 + 28 = 28 +

52 + 3 =   + 52   + 0 = 67   56 + 43 = 43 +

2 + 83 =   + 2   + 12 = 12   + 64 = 64 + 28

55 +   = 55   + 0 = 10   200 + 800 = 800 +

   + 0 = 647   8 + 0 =   345 + 871 =   + 345

Equations

Circle the correct number sentence.

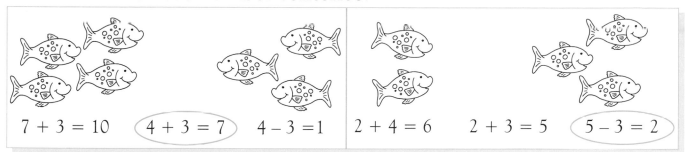

$7 + 3 = 10$　(4 + 3 = 7)　$4 - 3 = 1$　　　$2 + 4 = 6$　$2 + 3 = 5$　(5 - 3 = 2)

Circle the correct addition sentence.

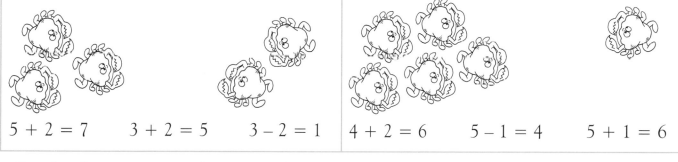

$5 + 2 = 7$　$3 + 2 = 5$　$3 - 2 = 1$　　$4 + 2 = 6$　$5 - 1 = 4$　$5 + 1 = 6$

Circle the correct subtraction sentence.

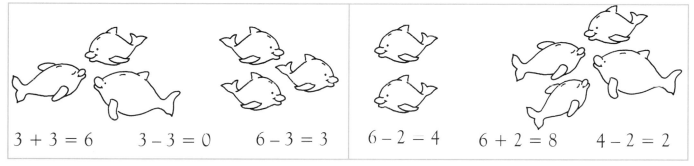

$3 + 3 = 6$　$3 - 3 = 0$　$6 - 3 = 3$　　$6 - 2 = 4$　$6 + 2 = 8$　$4 - 2 = 2$

Circle the correct number sentence.

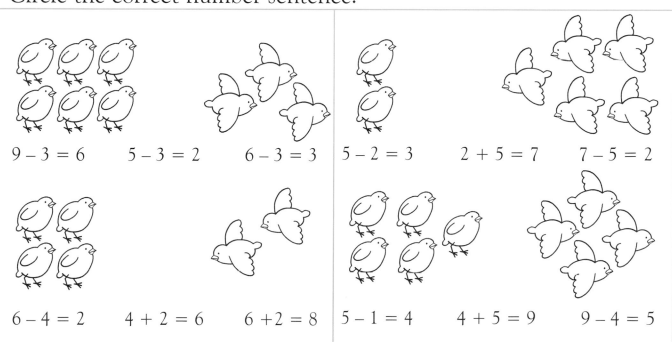

$9 - 3 = 6$　$5 - 3 = 2$　$6 - 3 = 3$　$5 - 2 = 3$　$2 + 5 = 7$　$7 - 5 = 2$

$6 - 4 = 2$　$4 + 2 = 6$　$6 + 2 = 8$　$5 - 1 = 4$　$4 + 5 = 9$　$9 - 4 = 5$

Picture graphs

Look at this picture graph. Then answer the questions.

Mina's marbles

Clear	◯	◯	◯	◯	◯
Blue	◯	◯	◯		
Green	◯	◯	◯	◯	
Red	◯	◯	◯		
Yellow	◯				

How many blue
marbles does Mina have?

Does Mina have more
green marbles or yellow marbles?

How many marbles
does Mina have in all?

Look at this picture graph. Then answer the questions.

Books on Pablo's shelf

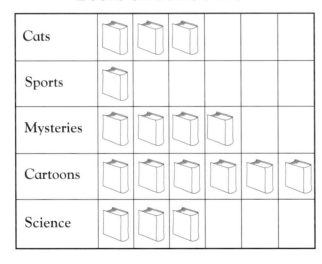

How many science
books does Pablo have?

Does he have more books
about cats than mysteries?

How many more cartoon books
does he have than mysteries?

How many books about
cats and science does he have?

Look at this picture graph. Then answer the questions.

Pets on Redmond Road

Cats	🐱	🐱	🐱	🐱			
Dogs	🐕	🐕	🐕	🐕	🐕		
Fish	🐟	🐟	🐟	🐟	🐟	🐟	🐟
Birds	🐦	🐦	🐦				

On Redmond Road,
are there more cats or dogs?

How many more
fish are there than dogs?

How many cats
and dogs are there?

How many pets are there in all?

3-dimensional shapes

Write the name of each shape.

 sphere

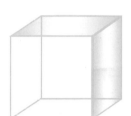 cube

Write the name of each shape. Use the words in the Word Box.

Word Box					
sphere	prism	cone	cube	cylinder	pyramid

prism

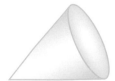

Missing addends

Write the missing addend.

6 + 7 = 13

Write the missing addend.

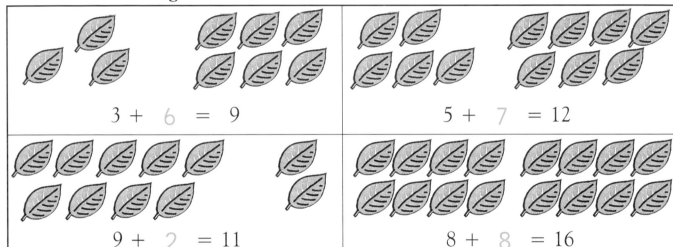

3 + 6 = 9

5 + 7 = 12

9 + 2 = 11

8 + 8 = 16

Write the missing addend.

3 + ___ = 7	5 + ___ = 14	9 + ___ = 12	8 + ___ = 10
7 + ___ = 12	7 + ___ = 15	7 + ___ = 12	9 + ___ = 17
7 + ___ = 13	8 + ___ = 14	10 + ___ = 13	4 + ___ = 13
4 + ___ = 7	3 + ___ = 9	2 + ___ = 11	8 + ___ = 13
6 + ___ = 8	5 + ___ = 9	7 + ___ = 8	8 + ___ = 12
8 + ___ = 9	6 + ___ = 13	8 + ___ = 16	5 + ___ = 11
4 + ___ = 11	10 + ___ = 15	8 + ___ = 11	4 + ___ = 10
7 + ___ = 14	8 + ___ = 15	9 + ___ = 14	6 + ___ = 15
9 + ___ = 16	9 + ___ = 18	3 + ___ = 10	5 + ___ = 9

Reading tables

Read the table. Then answer the questions.

Ages of cousins

NAME	AGE
Kinta	8
Paul	7
Clara	9
Meg	7
Lee	6

How old is Paul?

Who is older than Kinta?

Who is the same age as Meg?

Who is the youngest?

Read the table. Then answer the questions.

Favorite juice

Apple	6
Cranberry	2
Grape	3
Cherry	1
Orange	9

How many people
chose orange juice?

Which juice
did 2 people choose?

How many more people
like orange juice than apple juice?

Did more people choose
grape juice or cranberry juice?

Read the table. Then answer the questions.

Weight of dogs

NAME	Bear	Mike	Perry	Spike	Marca
POUNDS	64	13	20	11	6

Which dog weighs more than 50 pounds?

Which dog weighs less than 10 pounds?

How much more does Perry weigh than Mike?

How much less does Spike weigh than Mike?

Adding

Write the answer in the box.

```
   34          26          73
+  13       +  15       +  27
-------     -------     -------
   47          41         100
```

Write the answer in the box.

```
   45          31          53          62
+  24       +  18       +  26       +  16
-------     -------     -------     -------


   37          26          72          45
+  10       +  13       +  15       +  24
-------     -------     -------     -------


   39          24          52          36
+  10       +  15       +  17       +  13
-------     -------     -------     -------


   56          12          67          54
+  14       +  16       +  11       +  16
-------     -------     -------     -------


   48          64          36          55
+  12       +  14       +  13       +  15
-------     -------     -------     -------


   26          37          48          56
+  17       +  14       +  19       +  17
-------     -------     -------     -------


   28          64          56          38
+  16       +  26       +  27       +  23
-------     -------     -------     -------


   29          37          28          19
+  24       +  27       +  17       +  26
-------     -------     -------     -------


   26          36          46          34
+  38       +  76       +  44       +  66
-------     -------     -------     -------
```

Reading a calendar

Look at this calendar. Then answer the questions.

September

S	M	T	W	T	F	S
	1	2	3	4	5	6
7	8	9	10	11	12	13
14	15	16	17	18	19	20
21	22	23	24	25	26	27
28	29	30				

What day of the
week is the first day of
September on this calendar?

What date is the last
Tuesday in September?

Look at this calendar. Then answer the questions.

How many days are
in the month of July?

July

S	M	T	W	T	F	S
				1	2	3
4	5	6	7	8	9	10
11	12	13	14	15	16	17
18	19	20	21	22	23	24
25	26	27	28	29	30	31

What day of the week is the
last day of July on this calendar?

A camp starts on July 5
and ends on July 9. How
many camp days are there?

The campers go swimming
on Tuesday and Thursday.
On which dates will they swim?

Look at this calendar. Then answer the questions.

What date is the
first Sunday of November?

November

S	M	T	W	T	F	S
						1
2	3	4	5	6	7	8
9	10	11	12	13	14	15
16	17	18	19	20	21	22
23	24	25	26	27	28	29
30						

What day of the
week is November 14?

How many Saturdays
are shown in November?

Jenna's birthday is November 23.
What day of the week is it?

Subtracting

Write the answer in the box.

6 13		3 15		6 12
73		45		72
− 48		− 26		− 36
25		19		36

Write the answer in the box.

| 67 | 43 | 63 | 72 |
| − 48 | − 26 | − 46 | − 45 |

| 71 | 82 | 63 | 90 |
| − 47 | − 36 | − 44 | − 47 |

| 80 | 90 | 65 | 81 |
| − 46 | − 63 | − 37 | − 47 |

Write the answer in the box.

| 46 in. | 59 in. | 74 in. | 60 in. |
| − 18 in. | − 36 in. | − 27 in. | − 44 in. |

| 70 in. | 54 in. | 39 in. | 91 in. |
| − 47 in. | − 26 in. | − 4 in. | − 47 in. |

Write the answer in the box.

| 43¢ | 61¢ | 73¢ | 71¢ |
| − 17¢ | − 24¢ | − 36¢ | − 46¢ |

| 70¢ | 81¢ | 63¢ | 74¢ |
| − 44¢ | − 37¢ | − 46¢ | − 44¢ |

| 90 in. | 94 in. | 96 in. | 98 in. |
| − 34 in. | − 47 in. | − 78 in. | − 45 in. |

Properties of polygons

Circle the polygon that has the same number of sides.

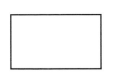 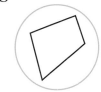   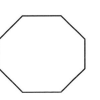

Circle the polygon that has the same number of sides.

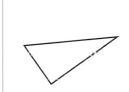 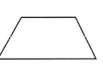 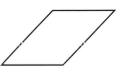

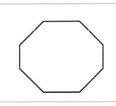 

Circle the polygon that has a different number of sides.

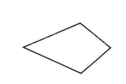

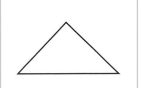   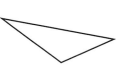

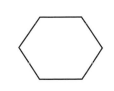

Venn diagrams

Read the clues to find the secret number.

1, 2, 3, 4, 5

3, 5, 7

It is in both the rectangle and the circle.

It is greater than 3.

What number is it?

Read the clues to find the secret number.

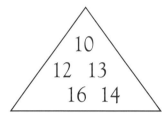

10
12 13
16 14

12   15
11   14
13

It is not in the square.
It is an even number.
It is less than 12.

What number is it?

10   11
12   13

13   14   15
20

11   12   13
20 15

It is in the rectangle and the circle.
It is greater than 13 and less than 20.
It is an odd number.

What number is it?

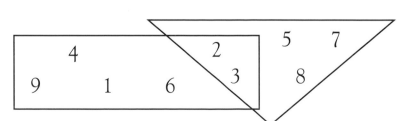

4   2   5   7
9   1   6   3   8

It is not an even number.
It is in the triangle.
It is in the rectangle.

What number is it?

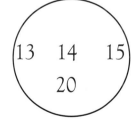

Most likely/least likely

Look at the marbles. Then answer the questions.

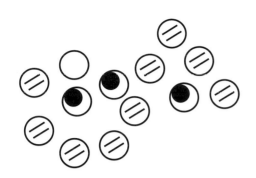

Which kind of marble would you be least likely to pick without looking?

Which kind of marble would you be most likely to pick without looking?

Look at the spinner. Then answer the questions.

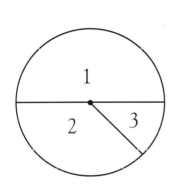

Is the spinner more likely to land on 1 or 2?

Is the spinner more likely to land on 2 or 3?

Which number is the spinner most likely to land on?

Which number is the spinner least likely to land on?

Look at the tally chart. Then answer the questions.

Imagine that each time you shake the bag, one coin falls out.

Tally of coins in the bag

COLOR	TALLIES
Pennies	IIII
Dimes	II
Nickels	Ж III
Quarters	Ж

Is a penny or a dime more likely to fall out?

Is a quarter or a nickel more likely to fall out?

Which coin is most likely to fall out?

Which coin is least likely to fall out?

3-dimensional shapes

Write the name of each shape.

Sphere

Cube

Write the name of each shape. Use the names in the Word Box.

Word Box

Sphere
Cube
Cylinder
Prism
Pyramid
Cone

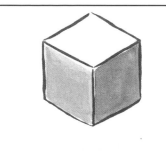

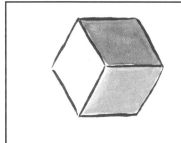

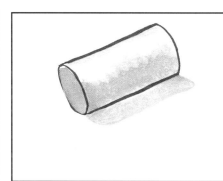

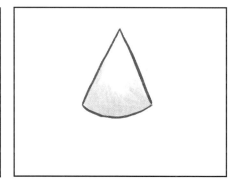

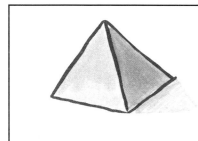

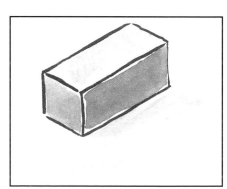

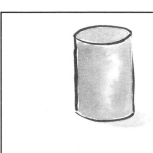

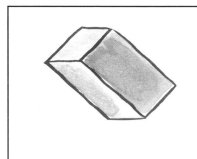

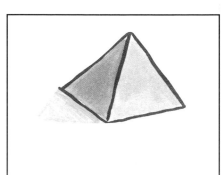

Counting

Write the missing number above each ↑.

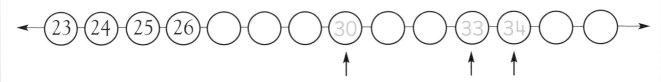

Write the missing number above each ↑.

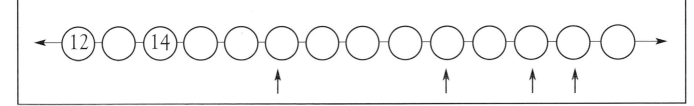

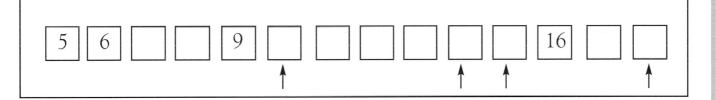

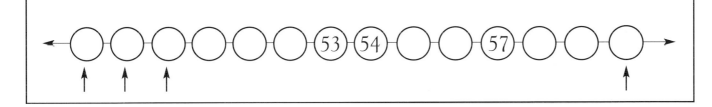

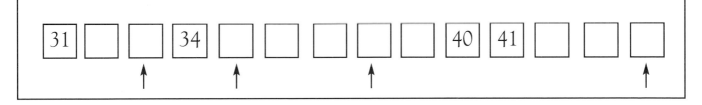

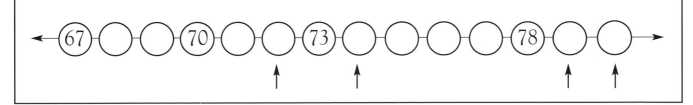

Finding patterns

Find the counting pattern. Write the missing numbers.

| 12 | 14 | 16 | 18 | 20 | 22 | 24 | 26 | 28 | 30 |

Find the counting pattern. Write the missing numbers.

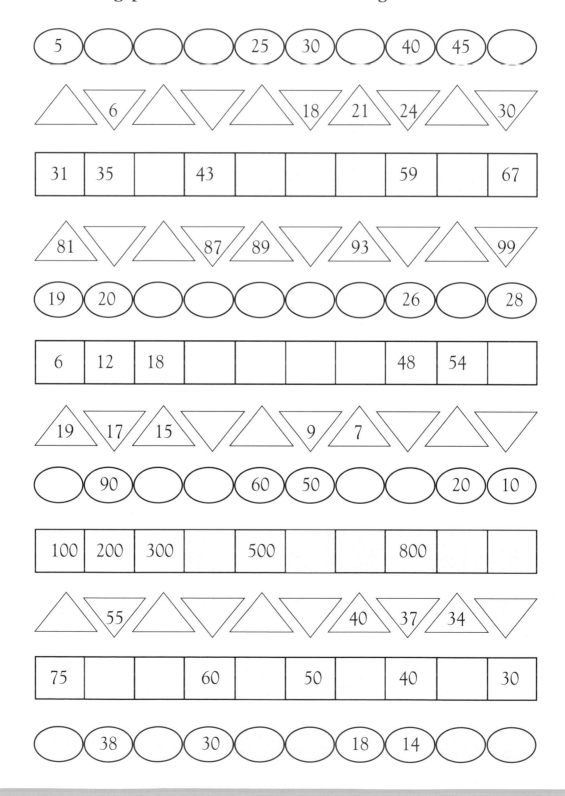

Reading tally charts

Look at the tally chart. Then answer the questions.

Winners at Tag

Kelly	Mark	Sandy	Rita	Brad
卌 ‖	‖‖	卌 ‖	卌	卌 ‖‖‖

Who won the most games?

Who won more games, Sandy or Kelly?

How many more games did Rita win than Mark?

Look at the tally chart. Then answer the questions.

Colors of T-Shirts sold

Blue	卌 卌 ‖
White	卌 ‖‖
Green	卌 ‖‖‖
Black	卌 卌 ‖

Which color shirt was sold most?

How many green shirts were sold?

Which color sold more, blue or green?

How many black shirts were sold?

How many more green shirts were sold than white shirts?

How many more black shirts were sold than green shirts?

How many T-shirts were sold in all?

Look at the tally chart. Then answer the questions.

Snack choices

Chips	Cherries	Cheese	Cookie	Apple
卌 ‖‖‖	卌	卌 卌 ‖	卌 ‖‖	卌 ‖

How many people chose chips?

Which snack did 7 people choose?

Did more people choose chips or cookies?

Which snack did the fewest people choose?

How many more people chose cheese than chips?

How many people chose apples and cherries?

Same shape and size

Which figure has same shape and size?

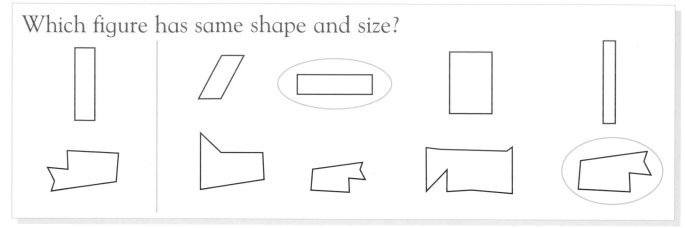

Circle the figure that has same shape and size.

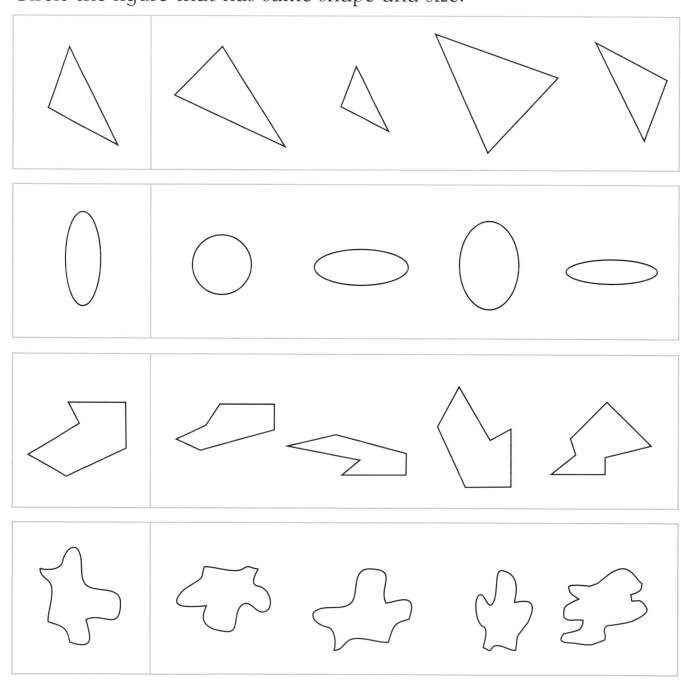

Parts of a set

Write the fraction that shows the shaded part of the set.
How many of the fish are shaded?

How many  ?   3

How many fish in all?   4

Write the fraction. $\dfrac{3}{4}$ part of the set
                                    whole set

Circle the fraction that shows the shaded part of the set.

$\dfrac{1}{3}$ $\dfrac{2}{3}$ $\dfrac{3}{2}$

$\dfrac{2}{3}$ $\dfrac{3}{5}$ $\dfrac{2}{5}$

$\dfrac{1}{4}$ $\dfrac{3}{4}$ $\dfrac{2}{4}$

$\dfrac{4}{5}$ $\dfrac{1}{5}$ $\dfrac{1}{4}$

Write the fraction that shows the shaded part of the set.

 $\dfrac{}{3}$

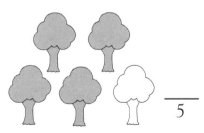 $\dfrac{}{5}$

 $\dfrac{}{4}$

 $\dfrac{}{5}$

 $\dfrac{}{7}$ $\dfrac{}{8}$

 $\dfrac{}{7}$

 $\dfrac{}{8}$ $\dfrac{}{6}$

Symmetry

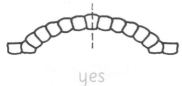 Hold a mirror along the dotted line. Does it show a line of symmetry?

yes   no   yes

Does the dotted line show a line of symmetry? Write yes or no.

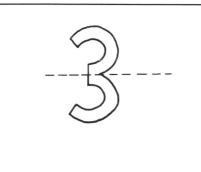

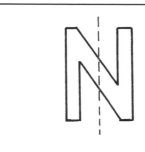

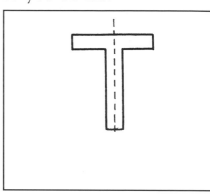

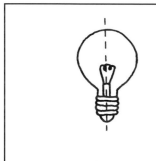

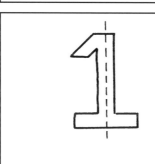

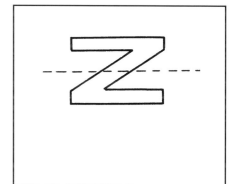

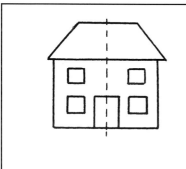

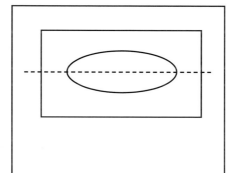

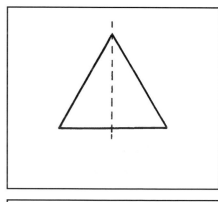

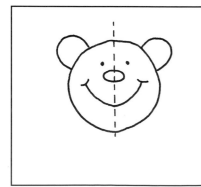

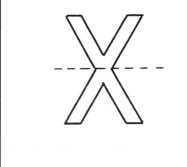

Measurement problems

Write the measurement
shown by the arrow.

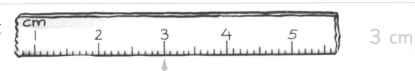

3 cm

Write the measurement shown by the arrow.

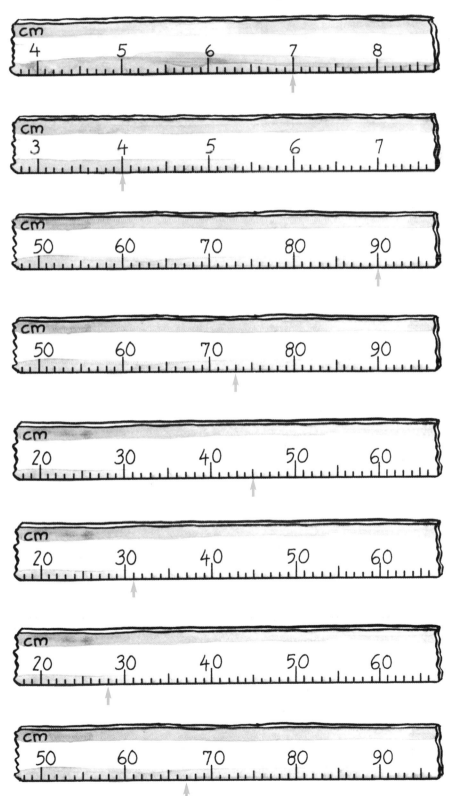

3-dimensional shapes

Write the name of each
shape in the box.

prism

sphere

Write the name of each shape in the box.

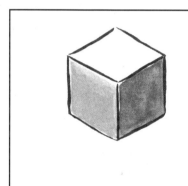

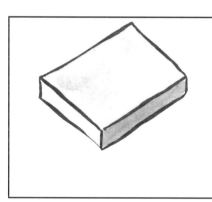

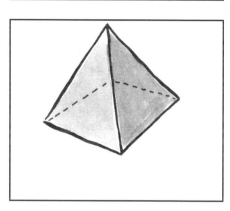

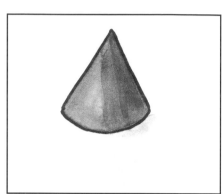

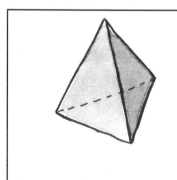

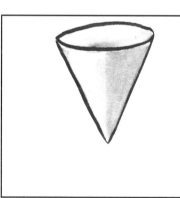

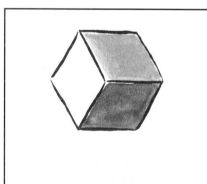

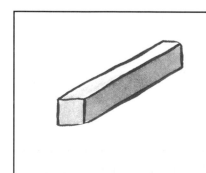

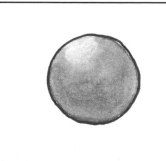

Answer Section with Parents' Notes

Grade 1
ages 6–7
Workbook

This section provides answers to all the activities in the book. These pages will enable you to mark your children's work, or they can be used by your children if they prefer to do their own marking.

The notes for each page help to explain common errors and problems and, where appropriate, indicate the kind of practice needed to ensure that your children understand where and how they have made errors.

2

Numbers
Trace the numbers.

0 1 2 3 4
5 6 7 8 9

Write the numbers.

```
0 0 0 0 0 0 0 0 0 0 0 0 0
1 1 1 1 1 1 1 1 1 1 1 1 1
2 2 2 2 2 2 2 2 2 2 2 2 2
3 3 3 3 3 3 3 3 3 3 3 3 3
4 4 4 4 4 4 4 4 4 4 4 4 4
5 5 5 5 5 5 5 5 5 5 5 5 5
6 6 6 6 6 6 6 6 6 6 6 6 6
7 7 7 7 7 7 7 7 7 7 7 7 7
8 8 8 8 8 8 8 8 8 8 8 8 8
9 9 9 9 9 9 9 9 9 9 9 9 9
```

Throughout Grade 1, children will need regular writing practice to reinforce the correct movement of the pencil. Watch out for numerals written backward and for any numeral written from the bottom up. All numerals should begin at the top.

3

Numbers and pictures
Count the animals, draw the dots, and write the number.

	2	[: :]	two
	3	[::.]	three
	5	[:.:]	five
	6	[::: :::]	six

Draw your own examples.

| | 1 | [·] | one |
| | 4 | [:. :.] | four |

At this stage, it is more important for children to be able to read the word for each number than to be able to spell it without help. Children can refer to the number line on the Progress Chart. Children can learn correct spellings gradually.

4

Counting
Connect each set to the correct number.

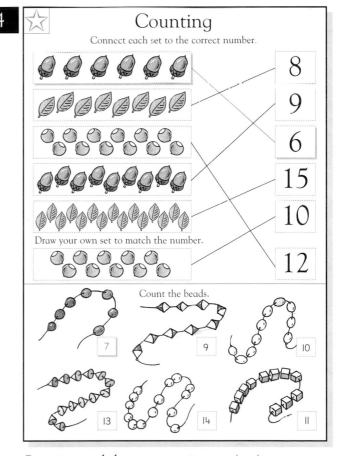

8
9
6
15
10
12

Draw your own set to match the number.

Count the beads.

7
9
10
13
14
11

Counting and then re-counting to check an answer before writing anything down is a useful habit to develop. Some children will be able to count without pointing to the objects, but when re-counting, children may need to point to each item.

Counting out loud
Say and write the missing numbers.

```
12        15    15        20
11        14    14        19
10        13    13        18
 9        12    12        17
 8        11    11        16
 7        10    10        15
 6         9     9        14
 5         8     8        13
 4         7     7        12
 3         6     6        11
 2         5     5        10
 1         4     4         9
 0         3     3         8
           2     2         7
           1     1         6
           0     0         5
                           4
                           3
                           2
                           1
                           0
```

```
0  1  2  3  4  5  6  7  8  9  10
11  12  13  14  15  16  17  18  19  20
```

It is important that children say the numbers out loud while completing each picture to reinforce the pattern of sounds that the numbers make. This will help them acquire a sense of whether the sequence sounds right. Make sure that zero is included here.

Missing numbers
Write in the missing numbers.

For snakes 4, 5 and 6, make sure that children writ 0 (zero) as the number nearest the tail and not 1. It is essential to encourage the use of the term *zero* and not *O* (as in *only*) or *nothing*. Have children look at the number line if they have problems.

Making 10
Color some fish green, and write the correct numbers in the boxes.

4 green 6 white
4 + 6 = 10

7 green 3 white
7 + 3 = 10

9 green 1 white
9 + 1 = 10

2 green 8 white
2 + 8 = 10

3 green 7 white
3 + 7 = 10

10 green 0 white
10 + 0 = 10

Write the missing numbers in the boxes to make 10.

```
10 +  0  = 10    6 +  4  = 10    2 +  8  = 10
 9 +  1  = 10    5 +  5  = 10    1 +  9  = 10
 8 +  2  = 10    4 +  6  = 10    0 + 10  = 10
 7 +  3  = 10    3 +  7  = 10
```

The number of items shaded and the number of items unshaded must match the numbers written in the answer boxes. For the bottom activity, find out whether children have noticed the pattern as it develops.

Count by 10s
Match the numbers to the words.

fifty   ten   thirty   twenty   forty

10 20 30 40 50 60 70 80 90 100

seventy   ninety   sixty   eighty   one hundred

Which numbers has the snail hidden?

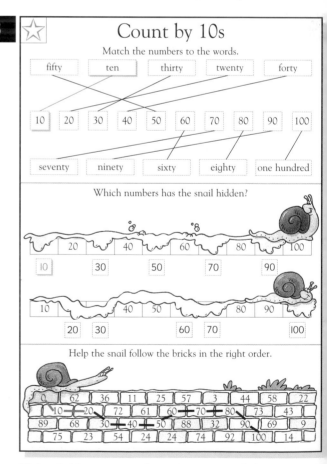

```
      20      40      60      80      100
10      30      50      70      90

      20      30      60  70      100
```

Help the snail follow the bricks in the right order.

```
 0  62  36  11  25  57   3  44  58  22
10  20  72  61  60  70  80  73  43
89  68  30  40  50  88  32  90  69   9
75  23  54  24  24  74  92  100  14
```

Help children recite the sequence and then say it ir reverse, from 100 back down to 10.

Count by 2s
Fill in the "hops" and circle the even numbers.

Color the even numbers.

1	2	3	4	5
6	7	8	9	10
11	12	13	14	15
16	17	18	19	20
21	22	23	24	25
26	27	28	29	30

Connect the dots in order.

Encourage children to read out loud the sequence of numbers they have found, e.g. 2, 4, 6, 8. For the grid activity (bottom left), make sure children notice the pattern. Point out that the shaded squares have even numbers and the others have odd numbers.

Patterns
Continue the pattern.

Make your own patterns.

Continue the number patterns.

2	4	6	2	4	6	2	4	6	2	4	6	2
10	9	9	10	9	9	10	9	9	10	9	9	10
1	3	5	7	1	3	5	7	1	3	5	7	1
5	5	5	6	5	5	5	6	5	5	5	6	5

Encourage children to talk about their own patterns and to explain what they have done. Explain that a mathematical pattern must have elements that repeat or progress in a predictable way.

Adding machines
Add the numbers, and write the answers.

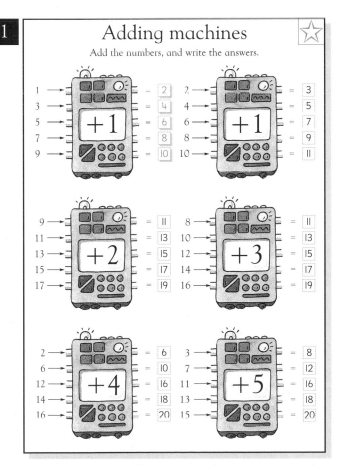

If children have difficulty with the exercises on the page, suggest to them that they use their fingers or counters to find the answers.

Reading numbers
Color enough things to match the number in each box.

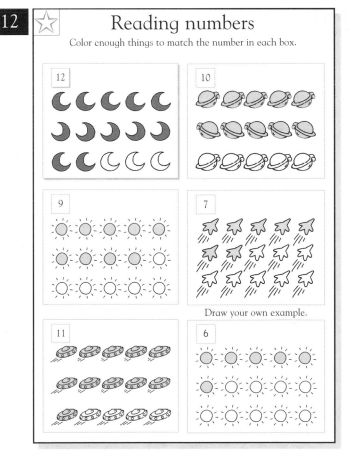

Draw your own example.

When checking the number of pictures children have colored, encourage them to go back and re-count the pictures aloud. Children might find it helpful to point to each picture as they count it.

Finding 10s
Ring 10 items, and write the numbers.

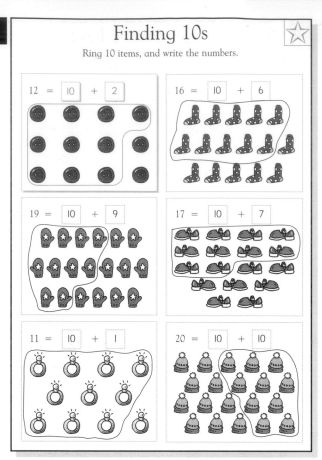

12 = 10 + 2

16 = 10 + 6

19 = 10 + 9

17 = 10 + 7

11 = 10 + 1

20 = 10 + 10

Make sure that each drawn ring does actually enclose 10 objects. If children ring any number of objects other than 10, they will arrive at an incorrect answer.

Tens and ones
How many tens and ones do you see?

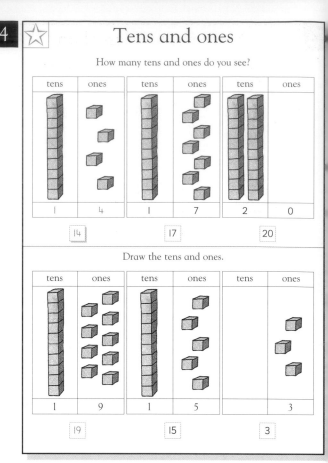

tens	ones
1	4

14

tens	ones
1	7

17

tens	ones
2	0

20

Draw the tens and ones.

tens	ones
1	9

19

tens	ones
1	5

15

tens	ones
	3

3

Make sure that children understand that the *1* in *14* stands for 1 ten, but the *1* in *41* represents 1 one

One more or one less?
Write one less and one more than the numbers shown in the boxes.

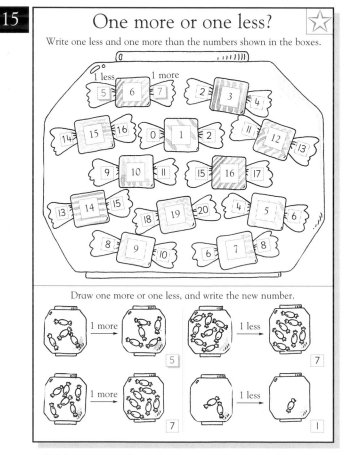

1 less   1 more

5 6 7

2 3 4

14 15 16

0 1 2

11 12 13

9 10 11

15 16 17

13 14 15

18 19 20

4 5 6

8 9 10

6 7 8

Draw one more or one less, and write the new number.

1 more   5

1 less   7

1 more   7

1 less   1

Children might benefit from making up their own number stories about the candies. For example, Rebecca had 3 candies, but her mother said she could have 1 more. Rebecca has 4 candies now.

Ordering
Color the prize ribbons.

4th= purple   3rd= yellow   1st= green   6th= red   2nd= blue   5th= orange

1st   2nd   3rd   4th   5th   6th

Which rabbit is 1st, 2nd, 3rd ...?

6th   5th   4th   3rd   2nd   1st

Which shape comes 1st, 2nd, 3rd ...?

Start here

● 3rd 8th
■ 2nd 7th
▮ 4th 9th
▲ 1st 6th
★ 5th 10th

Make sure that children understand the relationship between the numbers and the ordinals, that position 3 is 3rd, position 10 is 10th, and so on.

More than or less than?

Fill in the apples and numbers that make each sentence true.

5	is more than	3
5	is more than	2
8	is more than	6
12	is more than	4

Fill in the flowers and numbers to make each sentence true.

6	is less than	7
8	is less than	9
7	is less than	8
3	is less than	6

Children's answers will vary. Make sure that the number of objects drawn matches the numeral written in the box and that the number sentence is valid.

Greater or less?

Draw the hungry crocodiles.
They always eat the greater numbers!

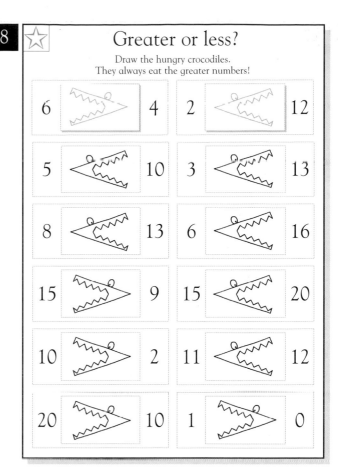

6	4	2	12
5	10	3	13
8	13	6	16
15	9	15	20
10	2	11	12
20	10	1	0

Make sure that children understand that the word *greater* means that one number is larger or higher in value than another. Make sure that children understand that even though 1 is a small number, it is greater than 0.

Comparing

heavier   lighter   bigger   smaller   longer   shorter

Draw the pictures to make each comparison true.

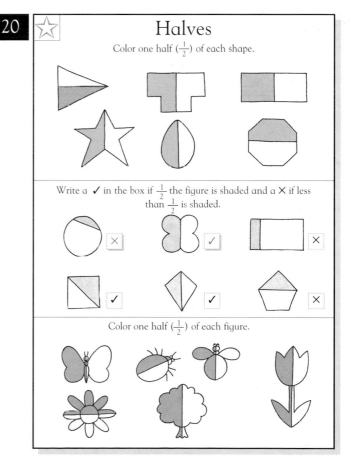

	heavier than	heavier than	
	lighter than	lighter than	
	bigger than	bigger than	
	smaller than	smaller than	
	longer than	longer than	
	shorter than	shorter than	

Make sure that children understand the kind of relationship among the three items that the comparative word describes.

Halves

Color one half ($\frac{1}{2}$) of each shape.

Write a ✓ in the box if $\frac{1}{2}$ the figure is shaded and a ✗ if less than $\frac{1}{2}$ is shaded.

✗   ✓   ✗
✓   ✓   ✗

Color one half ($\frac{1}{2}$) of each figure.

Make sure that children understand that the two halves of something must be exactly the same size.

Quarters

Color one quarter ($\frac{1}{4}$) of each shape.

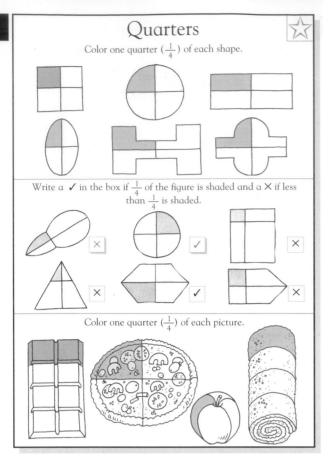

Write a ✔ in the box if $\frac{1}{4}$ of the figure is shaded and a ✗ if less than $\frac{1}{4}$ is shaded.

✗ ✔ ✗

✗ ✔ ✗

Color one quarter ($\frac{1}{4}$) of each picture.

Make sure children understand that the four quarters of something must be exactly the same size.

Adding up

Fill in the missing numbers, and add.

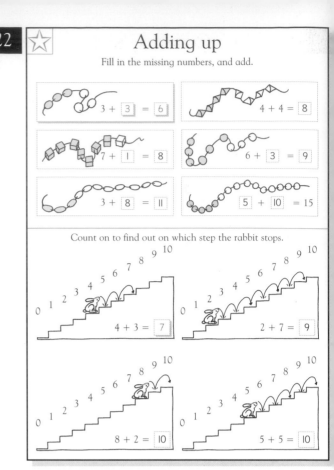

$3 + 3 = 6$ $4 + 4 = 8$

$7 + 1 = 8$ $6 + 3 = 9$

$3 + 8 = 11$ $5 + 10 = 15$

Count on to find out on which step the rabbit stops.

$4 + 3 = 7$ $2 + 7 = 9$

$8 + 2 = 10$ $5 + 5 = 10$

In the activity on top, the two numbers written must match the numbers of beads shaded and unshaded. In the last example, any one of a number of combinations could be correct. For the second activity, encourage your child to count mentally.

Adding animals

Count and add the animals, and then write the new number.

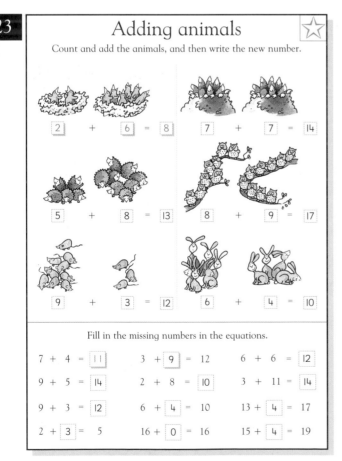

$2 + 6 = 8$ $7 + 7 = 14$

$5 + 8 = 13$ $8 + 9 = 17$

$9 + 3 = 12$ $6 + 4 = 10$

Fill in the missing numbers in the equations.

$7 + 4 = 11$ $3 + 9 = 12$ $6 + 6 = 12$

$9 + 5 = 14$ $2 + 8 = 10$ $3 + 11 = 14$

$9 + 3 = 12$ $6 + 4 = 10$ $13 + 4 = 17$

$2 + 3 = 5$ $16 + 0 = 16$ $15 + 4 = 19$

Children can solve these problems by counting on. They might also find it helpful to check their answers by using a number line.

Subtracting

Cross out the correct number of animals, and fill in the answers.

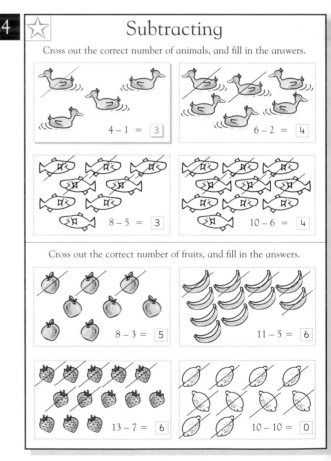

$4 - 1 = 3$ $6 - 2 = 4$

$8 - 5 = 3$ $10 - 6 = 4$

Cross out the correct number of fruits, and fill in the answers.

$8 - 3 = 5$ $11 - 5 = 6$

$13 - 7 = 6$ $10 - 10 = 0$

Make sure children understand the terms *cross out* and *left*. Guide children to see that crossing out a picture is a way of "taking away."

Counting back

Count back to find out on which step the frog stops.

$9 - 3 = \boxed{6}$

$5 - 1 = \boxed{4}$

$8 - 2 = \boxed{6}$

$7 - 0 = \boxed{7}$

$3 - 3 = \boxed{0}$

$10 - 8 = \boxed{2}$

Write the missing numbers in the boxes.

$3 - 3 = \boxed{0}$ $20 - 10 = \boxed{10}$ $9 - \boxed{3} = 6$ $15 - \boxed{10} = 5$

$5 - 4 = \boxed{1}$ $8 - 8 = \boxed{0}$ $5 - \boxed{5} = 0$ $20 - \boxed{16} = 4$

$15 - 4 = \boxed{11}$ $19 - 9 = \boxed{10}$ $6 - \boxed{4} = 2$ $18 - \boxed{7} = 11$

$10 - 9 = \boxed{1}$ $16 - 9 = \boxed{7}$ $10 - \boxed{6} = 4$ $13 - \boxed{3} = 10$

Make sure children understand that counting back is simply the reverse of counting on. Some children might find it helpful to use a number line to check the answers.

Sets

Write the missing numbers in the boxes.

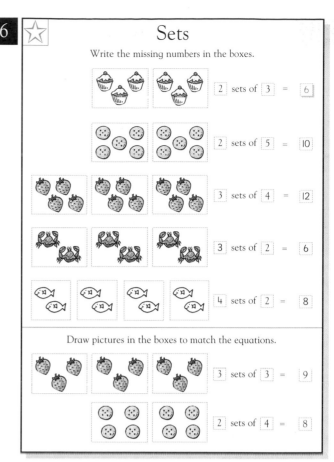

$\boxed{2}$ sets of $\boxed{3}$ = $\boxed{6}$

$\boxed{2}$ sets of $\boxed{5}$ = $\boxed{10}$

$\boxed{3}$ sets of $\boxed{4}$ = $\boxed{12}$

$\boxed{3}$ sets of $\boxed{2}$ = $\boxed{6}$

$\boxed{4}$ sets of $\boxed{2}$ = $\boxed{8}$

Draw pictures in the boxes to match the equations.

$\boxed{3}$ sets of $\boxed{3}$ = $\boxed{9}$

$\boxed{2}$ sets of $\boxed{4}$ = $\boxed{8}$

Talk with children about the pictures and what they show. If children have difficulties, make sure they haven't simply added the two numbers given beside the sets, e.g. 2 sets of 3 added together to make 5.

Money

Which coin?

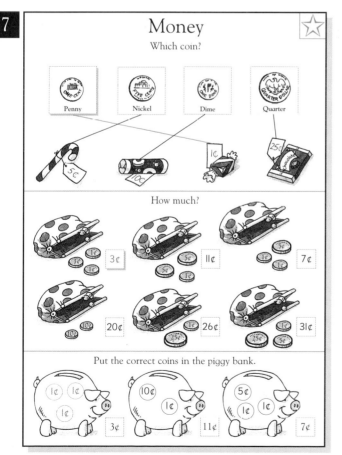

Penny   Nickel   Dime   Quarter

How much?

$3¢$ $11¢$ $7¢$

$20¢$ $26¢$ $31¢$

Put the correct coins in the piggy bank.

$3¢$ $11¢$ $7¢$

In the last activity, a number of combinations could be correct, and it might be helpful to re-count the amounts with children. For example: 1¢ 1¢ 1¢ 1¢ 1¢ 1¢ 1¢ or 5¢ 1¢ 1¢. Encourage children to use fewer coins when possible.

Ordering stories

Which happens 1st, 2nd, and 3rd?

2nd   3rd   1st

3rd   1st   2nd

3rd   2nd   1st

1st   2nd   3rd

Match the pictures to the order in which they happened.

4th   2nd   1st   3rd

Ask children to explain their reasons for each set of pictures in a particular way. If children have difficulty with the last set of pictures, point out that the girl's hair is dry when she is standing on the ladder into the pool.

Time

Write the time in each box.

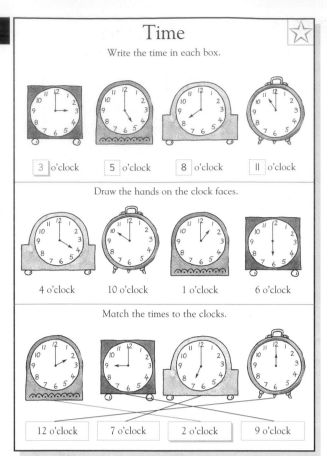

| 3 o'clock | 5 o'clock | 8 o'clock | 11 o'clock |

Draw the hands on the clock faces.

4 o'clock   10 o'clock   1 o'clock   6 o'clock

Match the times to the clocks.

| 12 o'clock | 7 o'clock | 2 o'clock | 9 o'clock |

Explain to children that when the hour hand (the short hand) points exactly to an hour, the minute hand (the long hand) should point exactly to 12 on the clock face.

Graphs

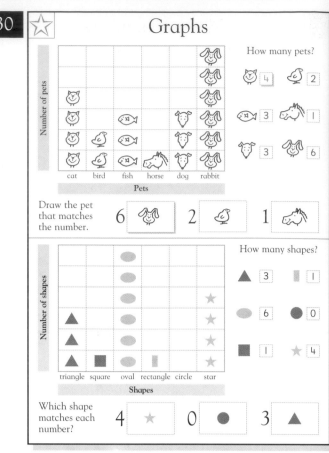

How many pets?

cat 🐱 4   bird 🐤 2
fish 🐟 3   horse 🐴 1
dog 🐑 3   rabbit 🐰 6

Draw the pet that matches the number.

6 🐕   2 🐤   1 🐴

How many shapes?

△ 3   ▌ 1
⬭ 6   ⬤ 0
◻ 1   ★ 4

Which shape matches each number?

4 ★   0 ●   3 ▲

Talk with children about the graphs and what they show. Discuss the numbers and labels on the graphs and what they mean. Explain that graphs show information that can be used to solve problems.

2-dimensional shapes

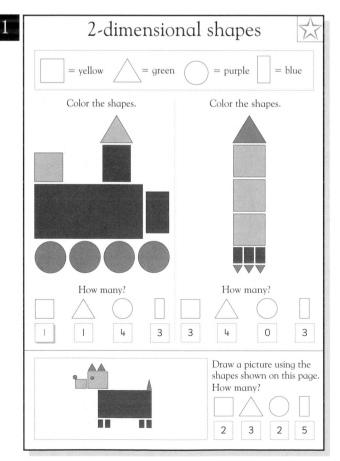

◻ = yellow   △ = green   ◯ = purple   ▮ = blue

Color the shapes.

Color the shapes.

How many?

| ◻ 1 | △ 1 | ◯ 4 | ▮ 3 |

How many?

| ◻ 3 | △ 4 | ◯ 0 | ▮ 3 |

Draw a picture using the shapes shown on this page. How many?

| ◻ 2 | △ 3 | ◯ 2 | ▮ 5 |

For the last activity, talk to children about their pictures. Encourage them to name each shape used and to state how many of each shape they used.

3-dimensional shapes

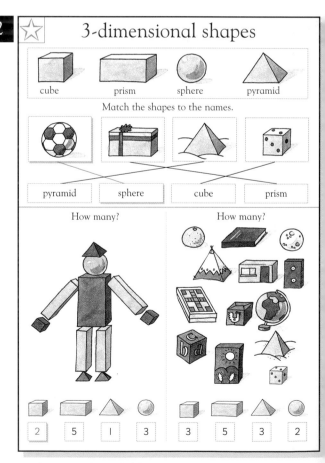

cube   prism   sphere   pyramid

Match the shapes to the names.

| pyramid | sphere | cube | prism |

How many?

How many?

| 2 | 5 | 1 | 3 |

| 3 | 5 | 3 | 2 |

Make sure that children recognize the same shapes when they are positioned differently. For example, they should recognize an upside-down pyramid.

Writing numbers

Count, write, and say the number of letters.

Christina	9	nine
Tarik	5	five
Grandpu	7	seven
Happy Birthday	13	thirteen
Good Morning Everyone	19	nineteen
How are you today?	14	fourteen

Write your name.

Make up your own message

Make sure that children understand they are to write the *number* of letters in the names and spell out the numbers. Praise their attempts if they are able to recognize letter patterns such as *teen* and use them to spell numbers such as *fourteen*, etc.

Counting

Write the missing numbers.

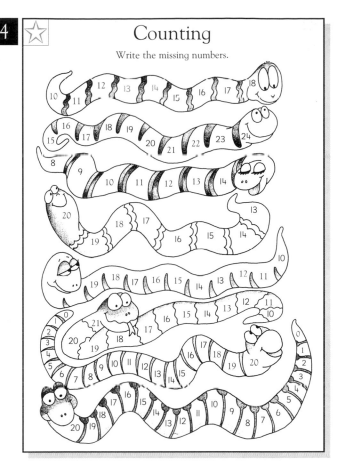

Some children may find it difficult to "cross over" a ten, e.g., from *19* to *20*, *21* and so on. Encourage them to see that after a number ends in *9*, the next number ends in *0*, and then the counting sequence begins again.

Counting on by 2s

Hop by 2s. Color the squares.

Elizabeth Even

Oliver Odd

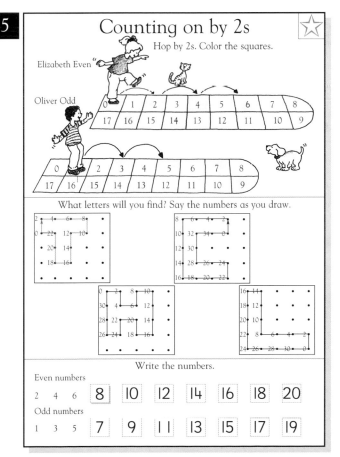

| 0 | 1 | 2 | 3 | 4 | 5 | 6 | 7 | 8 |
| | 17 | 16 | 15 | 14 | 13 | 12 | 11 | 10 | 9 |

| 0 | 2 | 3 | 4 | 5 | 6 | 7 | 8 |
| 17 | 16 | 15 | 14 | 13 | 12 | 11 | 10 | 9 |

What letters will you find? Say the numbers as you draw.

Write the numbers.

Even numbers

| 2 | 4 | 6 | 8 | 10 | 12 | 14 | 16 | 18 | 20 |

Odd numbers

| 1 | 3 | 5 | 7 | 9 | 11 | 13 | 15 | 17 | 19 |

Talk with children about the difference between Elizabeth Even's hops and Oliver Odd's hops. Tell them that counting by 2s is the same as counting every other number. Have children recite the sequences to become familiar with them.

Most and least

Circle the set with the most items in it.

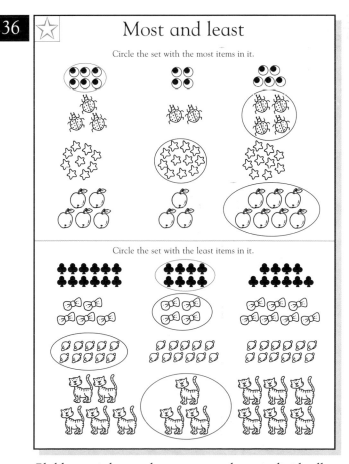

Circle the set with the least items in it.

Children might need to count each set individually to find out which of three sets of items has the most or the least. Children can use counters, if necessary.

Counting by 10s

Use this number line to help you.

0	10	20	30	40	50	60	70	80	90	100
zero	ten	twenty	thirty	forty	fifty	sixty	seventy	eighty	ninety	one hundred

How many candies? Count, say, and write.

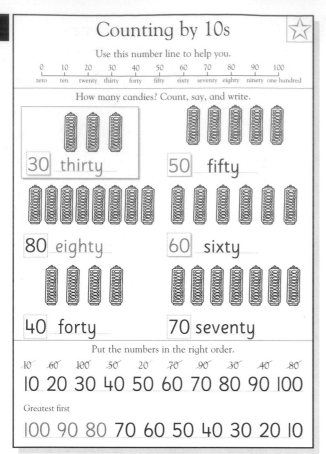

30 thirty   50 fifty

80 eighty   60 sixty

40 forty   70 seventy

Put the numbers in the right order.

~~10~~ ~~60~~ ~~100~~ ~~50~~ ~~20~~ ~~70~~ ~~90~~ ~~30~~ ~~40~~ ~~80~~

10 20 30 40 50 60 70 80 90 100

Greatest first

100 90 80 70 60 50 40 30 20 10

Point out the link between the sounds of some numbers, such as six and sixty, but also point out the exceptions. Check the spelling of *forty* (not *fourty*). Also point out that 100 is *one hundred*, not *ten-ty*, and 20 is *twenty*, not *two-ty*.

Counting forward or back

Draw pathways by writing the missing numbers.

If children have difficulty, let them work with a number line, using both hands. Tell them to keep one finger on the number they are starting from and to use the other hand to count. This way, they will not count the starting number.

Reading numbers

Connect the numbers, and complete the drawings.

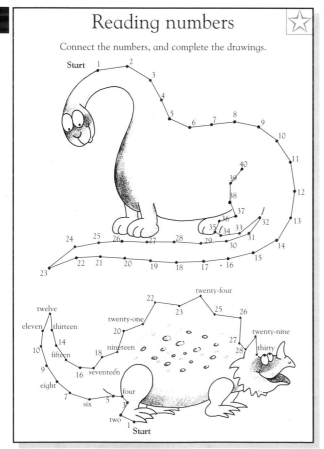

Encourage children to use the counting sequence to help them connect the numbers. For the second picture, help students to see that the counting sequence is the same, but some of the numbers are words.

Tens and ones

Write the tens and ones.

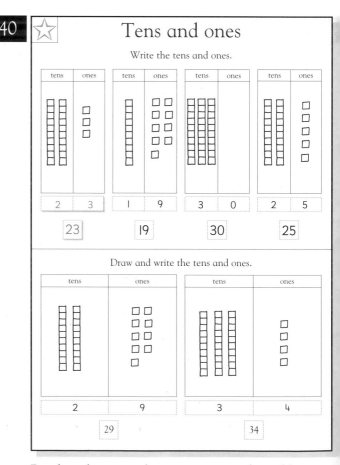

tens	ones
2	3

23

tens	ones
1	9

19

tens	ones
3	0

30

tens	ones
2	5

25

Draw and write the tens and ones.

tens	ones
2	9

29

tens	ones
3	4

34

Breaking large numbers into parts makes adding them easier. So, 22 + 14 becomes 20 + 2 + 10 + 4. Adding the ones first gives 2 + 4 = 6 and the tens next gives 20 + 10 = 30. The two partial answers can then be combined to give 30 + 6 = 36.

Comparisons

Add the values, and write *is greater than* or *is less than*.

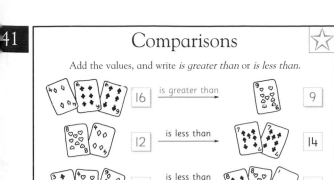

16 → is greater than → 9

12 → is less than → 14

16 → is less than → 17

16 → is greater than → 13

Write the numbers that are 1 more, 1 less, or between.

1 less	between	1 more	1 less	number	1 more
20	21	22	25	26	27

number	between	number	1 less	number	1 more
19	20	21	28	29	30

1 less	number	1 more	number	between	number
10	11	12	30	31	32

Children should make use of addition facts to determine totals. If they manage the greater-than and less-than part of the page well, they could then find out how much greater or less one number is than another.

Comparing money

Color the one who has the most money.

Draw some coins in the purses.

is less than — 5¢ — is less than — (10¢)

is less than — 14¢ — is less than — (10¢ 10¢)

is less than — 20¢ — is less than — (25¢ 1¢)

Answers for the lower activity will vary. Make sure that the amount children assign to the first purse is less than the amount on the tag and that the amount children assign to the second purse is greater than that on the tag.

Spot the doubles

Draw the missing spots and write the numbers.

3 + 3 = 6
double 3 is 6

4 + 4 = 8
double 4 is 8

1 + 1 = 2
double 1 is 2

2 + 2 = 4
double 2 is 4

6 + 6 = 12
double 6 is 12

5 + 5 = 10
double 5 is 10

7 + 7 = 14
double 7 is 14

10 + 10 = 20
double 10 is 20

Encourage children to become familiar with doubles. These facts can then be used in other situations, such as "doubles plus 1."

---

10 more or 10 less

Draw a line to add 10 to each number on the rocket.

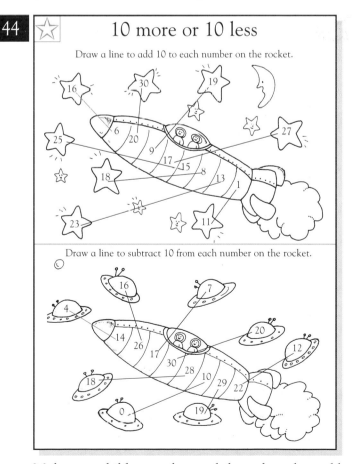

Draw a line to subtract 10 from each number on the rocket.

Make sure children understand that when they add 10 or subtract 10, they must work with the tens. Familiarity with "10 more" and "10 less" will help to develop the ability to do mental math.

Ordinals

Color the beads.

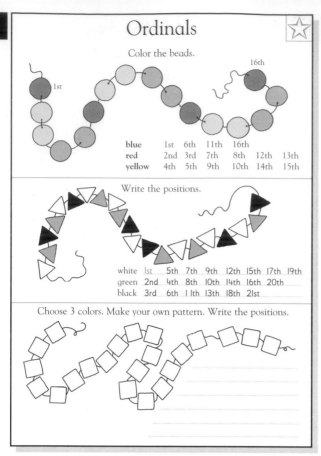

blue	1st	6th	11th	16th
red	2nd	3rd	7th	8th	12th	13th
yellow	4th	5th	9th	10th	14th	15th

Write the positions.

white	1st	5th	7th	9th	12th	15th	17th	19th
green	2nd	4th	8th	10th	14th	16th	20th
black	3rd	6th	11th	13th	18th	21st

Choose 3 colors. Make your own pattern. Write the positions.

Make sure children understand that the sequence of ordinals is the same as the basic counting sequence.

Ordering

Look for a pattern. Write the numbers in order.

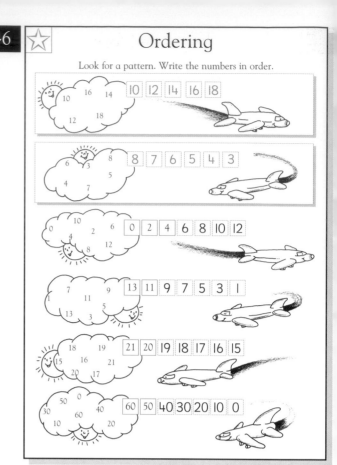

10	12	14	16	18

8	7	6	5	4	3

0	2	4	6	8	10	12

13	11	9	7	5	3	1

21	20	19	18	17	16	15

60	50	40	30	20	10	0

Make sure children understand that some of the patterns require counting on and some require counting back. Children should see that some patterns are familiar, such as counting by 2s, counting by 10s, and the basic counting sequence.

Halves and fourths

For each shape color one half red or one fourth yellow.

Halves or fourths?

$\frac{1}{2}$ $\frac{1}{4}$ $\frac{1}{2}$ $\frac{1}{2}$ $\frac{1}{2}$ $\frac{1}{4}$

Make sure that children understand that halves must be two exactly equal parts and that fourths must be four exactly equal parts. Encourage children to see that two fourths are the same as one half.

Place value

What is in the ones place in each number?

24	461	87	119
4	1	7	9

365	68	13	842
5	8	3	2

What is in the tens place in each number?

30	594	10	769
3	9	1	6

127	81	18	150
2	8	1	5

What is in the hundreds place in each number?

124	907	436	580
1	9	4	5

Circle the number that has a 7 in the tens place.

457   794   870

Circle the number that has a 3 in the ones place.

134   693   308

Circle the number that has a 1 in the hundreds place.

106   610   421

Make sure children understand that the ones are at the right of a number. Children should then see that the tens are just to the left of the ones, and the hundreds are just to the left of the tens.

Expanded form

Write each number as a sum of tens and ones.

54 = 50 + 4   12 = 10 + 2   88 = 80 + 8

47 = 40 + 7   29 = 20 + 9   11 = 10 + 1

75 = 70 + 5   51 = 50 + 1   44 = 40 + 4

62 = 60 + 2   93 = 90 + 3   19 = 10 + 9

25 = 20 + 5   74 = 70 + 4   36 = 30 + 6

Write the missing number.

80 + 6 = 86   90 + 7 = 97

30 + 3 = 33   60 + 1 = 61

10 + 5 = 15   50 + 8 = 58

20 + 2 = 22   70 + 9 = 79

40 + 3 = 43   90 + 4 = 94

Children should be able to apply what they know about place value to help them to understand expanded form. Make sure that children correctly break numbers apart into tens and ones.

Adding dice

Count the dots on the dice.

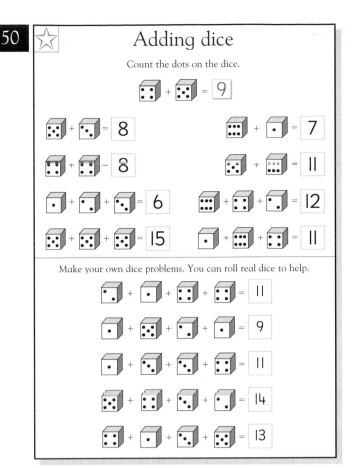

Make your own dice problems. You can roll real dice to help.

Children can use addition facts to find the answers for the first section. Their answers will vary for the second section. Possible answers are given.

Adding

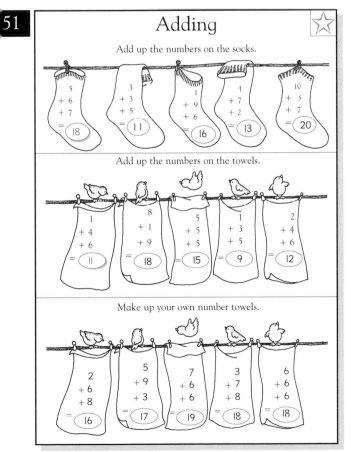

Add up the numbers on the socks.

Add up the numbers on the towels.

Make up your own number towels.

Encourage children to use addition facts to help them to find the totals. Facts that produce the total 10 are particularly helpful.

Crossing out

Cross out one type of shape in each box.

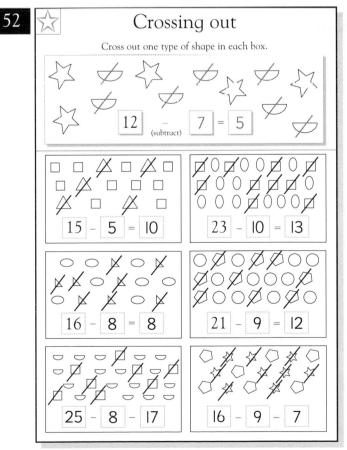

12 − 7 = 5
(subtract)

15 − 5 = 10   23 − 10 = 13

16 − 8 = 8   21 − 9 = 12

25 − 8 = 17   16 − 9 = 7

It doesn't matter which set of shapes children choose to cross out. Point out that crossing out pictures is like subtracting these objects. Answers will vary, depending on which set of shapes children cross out.

Subtraction

Say and count as you write.

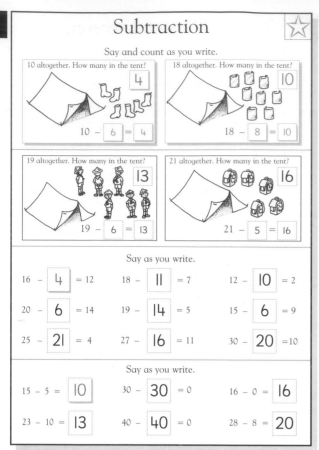

10 altogether. How many in the tent?

$10 - \boxed{6} = 4$

18 altogether. How many in the tent?

$18 - \boxed{8} = 10$

19 altogether. How many in the tent?

$19 - \boxed{6} = 13$

21 altogether. How many in the tent?

$21 - \boxed{5} = 16$

Say as you write.

$16 - \boxed{4} = 12 \qquad 18 - \boxed{11} = 7 \qquad 12 - \boxed{10} = 2$

$20 - \boxed{6} = 14 \qquad 19 - \boxed{14} = 5 \qquad 15 - \boxed{6} = 9$

$25 - \boxed{21} = 4 \qquad 27 - \boxed{16} = 11 \qquad 30 - \boxed{20} = 10$

Say as you write.

$15 - 5 = \boxed{10} \qquad 30 - \boxed{30} = 0 \qquad 16 - 0 = \boxed{16}$

$23 - 10 = \boxed{13} \qquad 40 - \boxed{40} = 0 \qquad 28 - 8 = \boxed{20}$

Have children recall fact families for help in solving problems such as 21 − 5 = 16 and 21 − 16 = 5. Remind children that a number subtracted from itself gives a difference of zero.

Sets of

Say and count as you write.

$4 + 4 + 4 = \boxed{12}$ legs

$\boxed{3}$ sets of $\boxed{4} \longrightarrow \boxed{12}$

$8 + 8 = \boxed{16}$ legs

$\boxed{2}$ sets of $\boxed{8} \longrightarrow \boxed{16}$

$5 + 5 + 5 + 5 = \boxed{20}$ legs

$\boxed{4}$ sets of $\boxed{5} \longrightarrow \boxed{20}$

$3 + 3 + 3 + 3 = \boxed{12}$ legs

$\boxed{4}$ sets of $\boxed{3} \longrightarrow \boxed{12}$

$2 + 2 + 2 = \boxed{6}$ legs

$\boxed{3}$ sets of $\boxed{2} \longrightarrow \boxed{6}$

$10 + 10 = \boxed{20}$ legs

$\boxed{2}$ sets of $\boxed{10} \longrightarrow \boxed{20}$

Talk with children about the pictures and what they show. If children have difficulty, make sure that they haven't simply added the two numbers given below the sets: for example, 3 sets of 4 added together to make 7.

Sharing

Share the food equally.

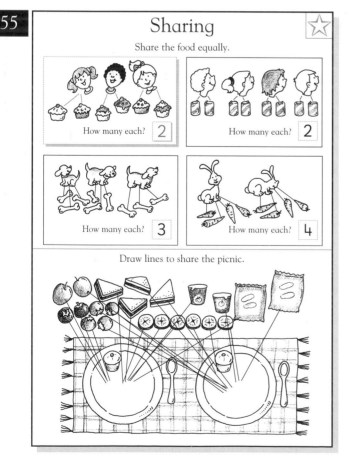

How many each? $\boxed{2}$

How many each? $\boxed{2}$

How many each? $\boxed{3}$

How many each? $\boxed{4}$

Draw lines to share the picnic.

Encourage the use of the word *sharing*. Lead children to understand that sharing means separating a group of items into smaller, equal-size groups. For example, 3 dogs sharing 9 bones gives 3 bones to each dog.

Addition properties

Write the missing number.

$6 + \boxed{0} = 6 \qquad\qquad \boxed{0} + 6 = 6$

$10 + 7 = 17 \qquad\qquad 7 + \boxed{10} = 17$

$11 + \boxed{0} = 11 \qquad\qquad 0 + \boxed{11} = 11$

$4 + 8 = \boxed{12} \qquad\qquad 8 + \boxed{4} = 12$

$13 + 6 = \boxed{19} \qquad\qquad 6 + 13 = 19$

$0 + \boxed{3} = 3 \qquad\qquad 3 + \boxed{0} = 3$

Circle the addition fact that has the same sum as 2 + 3.

$1 + 5 \qquad \boxed{(3 + 2)} \qquad 4 + 2$

Circle the addition fact that has the same sum as 5 + 8.

$\boxed{(8 + 5)} \qquad 6 + 6 \qquad 3 + 9$

Circle the addition fact that has the same sum as 1 + 7.

$8 + 2 \qquad 2 + 5 \qquad \boxed{(7 + 1)}$

Circle the addition fact that has the same sum as 10 + 6.

$7 + 4 \qquad 9 + 9 \qquad \boxed{(6 + 10)}$

Circle the addition fact that has the same sum as 4 + 2.

$1 + 6 \qquad \boxed{(2 + 4)} \qquad 3 + 2$

Circle the addition fact that has the same sum as 9 + 5.

$\boxed{(5 + 9)} \qquad 7 + 6 \qquad 10 + 5$

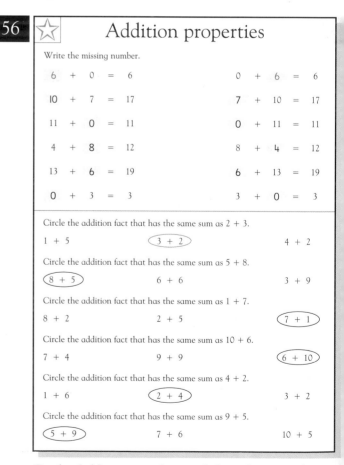

Guide children to understand that the sum of zero and any number is that number. Also, the sum of any two numbers is the same, no matter which of the numbers comes first.

Most and least likely

What are you most likely to pick out of each bag? Circle the answer.

What are you least likely to pick out of each bag? Circle the answer.

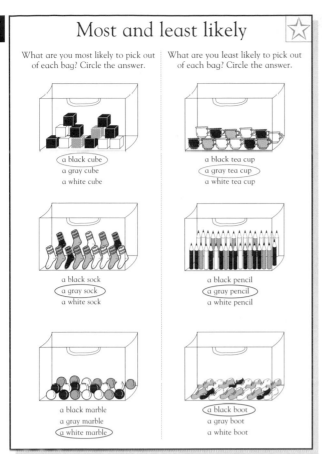

a black cube
(a gray cube)
a white cube

a black tea cup
(a gray tea cup)
a white tea cup

a black sock
(a gray sock)
a white sock

a black pencil
(a gray pencil)
a white pencil

a black marble
a gray marble
(a white marble)

(a black boot)
a gray boot
a white boot

Children should understand that the most likely item is the item of which there are the most and that the least likely item is the item of which there are the fewest.

Days and seasons

Days of the week
Can you write them in order?

Monday Tuesday Wednesday Thursday Friday Saturday Sunday

Wednesday Thursday Friday Saturday Sunday Monday Tuesday

Saturday Sunday Monday Tuesday Wednesday Thursday Friday

Thursday Friday Saturday Sunday Monday Tuesday Wednesday

Yesterday and tomorrow

yesterday	today	tomorrow
Tuesday	Wednesday	Thursday
Sunday	Monday	Tuesday
Wednesday	Thursday	Friday
Saturday	Sunday	Monday

Seasons of the year
Draw lines to connect each picture to a season.

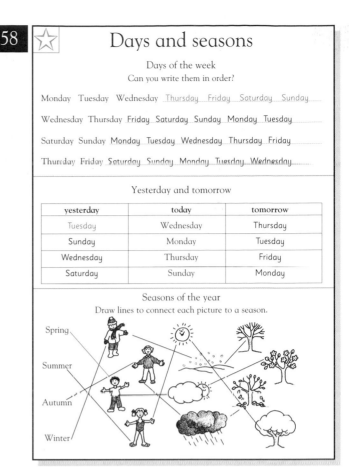

Spring
Summer
Autumn
Winter

Children need to know the order of the days. They should also know that the name of each day begins with a capital letter. Ask children to explain their reasons for connecting the season pictures the way they did.

Using clocks

Write the time.

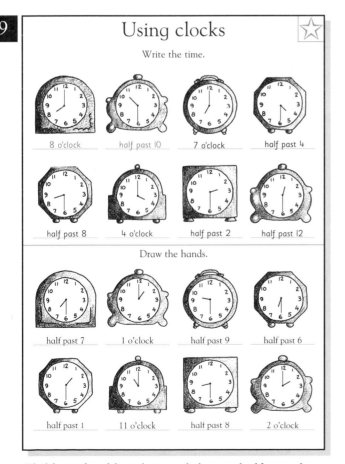

8 o'clock   half past 10   7 o'clock   half past 4

half past 8   4 o'clock   half past 2   half past 12

Draw the hands.

half past 7   1 o'clock   half past 9   half past 6

half past 1   11 o'clock   half past 8   2 o'clock

Children should understand that at half past the hour, the long hand (the minute hand) must point to the 6 on the clock face.

Favorite fruits

This table shows the favorite fruits of a class of children.

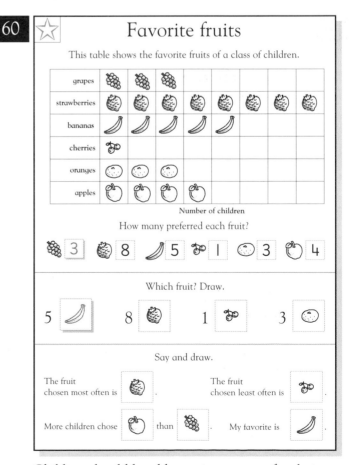

grapes								
strawberries								
bananas								
cherries								
oranges								
apples								

Number of children

How many preferred each fruit?

🍇 3   🍓 8   🍌 5   🍒 1   🍊 3   🍎 4

Which fruit? Draw.

5 🍌   8 🍓   1 🍒   3 🍊

Say and draw.

The fruit chosen most often is 🍓 .

The fruit chosen least often is 🍒 .

More children chose 🍎 than 🍇 .

My favorite is 🍌

Children should be able to give reasons for their choices. Make sure they understand that each individual drawing of a fruit or a bunch of fruit on the table stands for one child in the class.

Draw the other half

Finish the pictures.

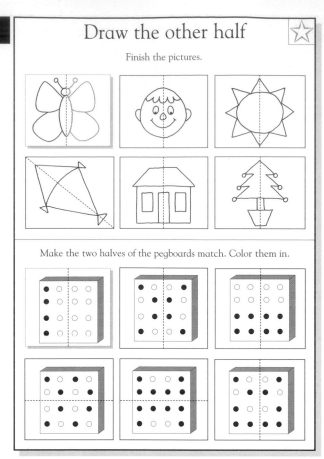

Make the two halves of the pegboards match. Color them in.

Placing a small mirror along the line of symmetry will enable children to see the complete image. For the second activity, it is important to understand that the unmarked half should be a mirror image of the marked half.

Where's the bear?

| on | yes |
| next to | no |

| inside | no |
| on top | yes |

| inside | no |
| up | yes |

| behind | no |
| beside | yes |

| on | no |
| in | yes |

| in front | yes |
| inside | no |

| under | no |
| behind | yes |

| above | no |
| under | yes |

| on | yes |
| over | no |

| down | yes |
| up | no |

Read the words with children before they do the page. Point out that sometimes more than one term may describe similar positions. For example, *above* can sometimes be used in place of *on top*.

Numbers

Write the numbers.

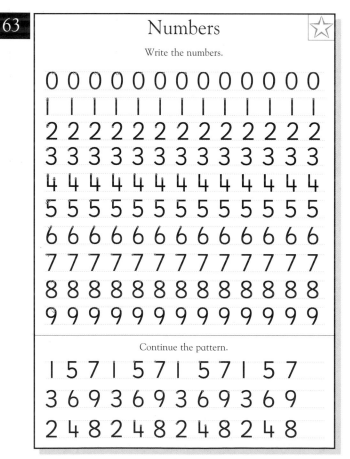

0 0 0 0 0 0 0 0 0 0 0 0 0
1 1 1 1 1 1 1 1 1 1 1 1 1
2 2 2 2 2 2 2 2 2 2 2 2 2
3 3 3 3 3 3 3 3 3 3 3 3 3
4 4 4 4 4 4 4 4 4 4 4 4 4
5 5 5 5 5 5 5 5 5 5 5 5 5
6 6 6 6 6 6 6 6 6 6 6 6 6
7 7 7 7 7 7 7 7 7 7 7 7 7
8 8 8 8 8 8 8 8 8 8 8 8 8
9 9 9 9 9 9 9 9 9 9 9 9 9

Continue the pattern.

1 5 7 1 5 7 1 5 7 1 5 7
3 6 9 3 6 9 3 6 9 3 6 9
2 4 8 2 4 8 2 4 8 2 4 8

Children need to practice writing numbers correctly. Explain to children that they should write each number beginning from the top of the number.

Numbers

Which numbers are the snakes hiding?
Say the numbers as you write the answers.

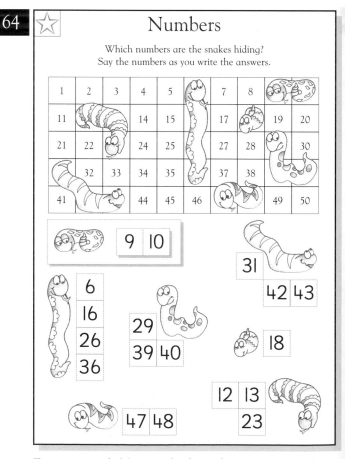

1	2	3	4	5		7	8		
11			14	15		17		19	20
21	22		24	25		27	28		30
	32	33	34	35		37	38		
41			44	45	46			49	50

9 10

31

42 43

6
16
26
36

29
39 40

18

12 13
23

47 48

Encourage children to look at the patterns in the numbers as they read down columns. They should also know the basic counting sequence. Make sure children understand that a snake can hide numbers that do not form a sequence.

Addition

How many are there in all? Color them in.

Children may either count to find the total or determine the number of items on either side of the addition symbol and add the two numbers to find the total.

1 less or 1 more

Count, draw, and write.

Children should understand that *1 less* means that they should subtract 1 and that *1 more* means that they should add 1. Help them, if necessary, to cross tens, such as adding 1 more to 79.

Tallies

Which tally marks show 13?

Which tally marks show 15?

Which tally marks show 17?

Which tally marks show 23?

Make sure children understand that each complete tally-mark set represents 5. Children can then determine totals by counting by 5s and then counting on.

Using a table

Use the table to answer the questions.
Circle the correct answer.

Glasses of water		
Name	Saturday	Sunday
Sasha	4	6
William	6	4
Anita	6	8
Nabi	5	7

Who drank less water on Saturday?   (Sasha) Nabi

How many glasses of water did Anita drink on Sunday?   4   (8)   7

Who drank 7 glasses of water on Sunday?   (Nabi) Anita

Who drank a total of 10 glasses of water?   Nabi (William)

Who drank the most glasses of water?   Nabi (Anita)

Who drank less water on Sunday?   Anita (Nabi)

How many glasses of water did Sasha and William together drink on Saturday?   (10)   12

If children have difficulty reading the names in the table, point out to them that they can identify the names in the questions by matching them with the spellings of the names in the table.

Patterns of 2, 5, and 10

Count, color, and find a pattern.

Count by 2s and color them green.

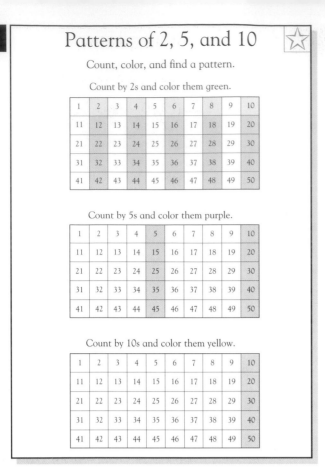

Count by 5s and color them purple.

Count by 10s and color them yellow.

Discuss the patterns made. Ask children to look for any numbers that are colored in all the patterns. (The 10s will be.) Guide children to see that all the numbers in the pattern formed by counting by 5s end in a 5 or a 0.

More or less

Connect the spaceships to the planets and the rockets to the stars.

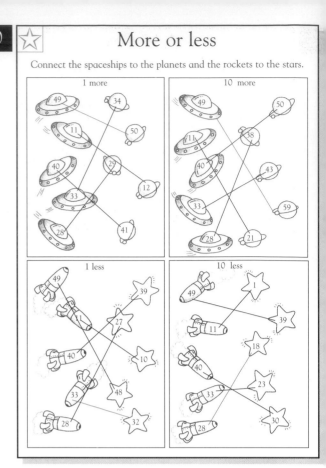

1 more

10 more

1 less

10 less

Discuss the changes for each set of numbers. Point out to children that, in some cases, both the tens digit and the ones digit change. Remind children that *more* means they must add and that *less* means they must subtract.

Ordering

Write the numbers in order.

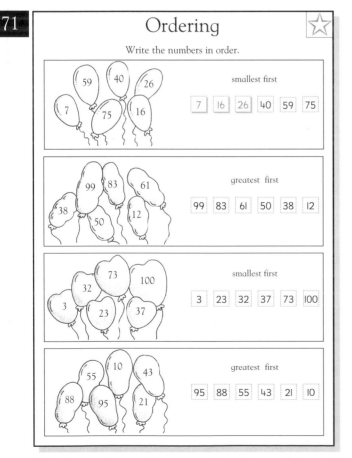

smallest first

| 7 | 16 | 26 | 40 | 59 | 75 |

greatest first

| 99 | 83 | 61 | 50 | 38 | 12 |

smallest first

| 3 | 23 | 32 | 37 | 73 | 100 |

greatest first

| 95 | 88 | 55 | 43 | 21 | 10 |

Watch out for possible reversals such as reading 16 as 61. In the third section, 23, 32, 37, and 73 have been included to deal with such reversals. Ask children to identify the place values of the digits in 37 and 73.

Fractions of shapes

Color one-third ($\frac{1}{3}$).

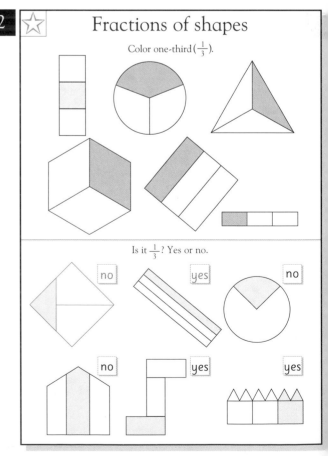

Is it $\frac{1}{3}$? Yes or no.

no   yes   no

no   yes   yes

Explain why some of the pictures in the second section do not show one third, even though each shape is cut into three pieces. (The pieces are not all of equal size.)

Addition

How many are there in all? Color them in.

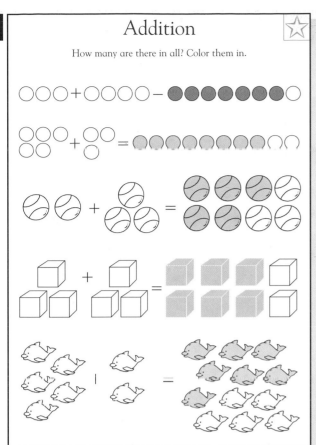

Suggest to children that they write the number of items below each group on either side of the addition symbol. When they find the total, they can write that number under the items they have colored in.

Adding coins

Use three coins each time.
How many different totals can you make?

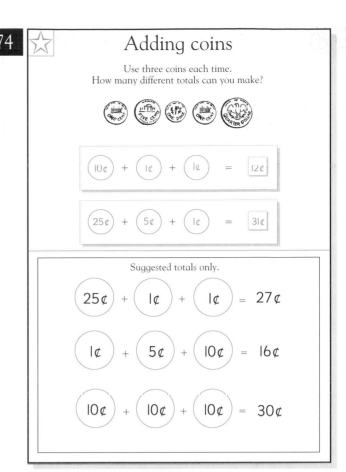

Encourage children to keep track of the different combinations of coins that they use. In this way, they can avoid repeating combinations.

Addition grid

Draw rings around the pairs of numbers that add up to 20.

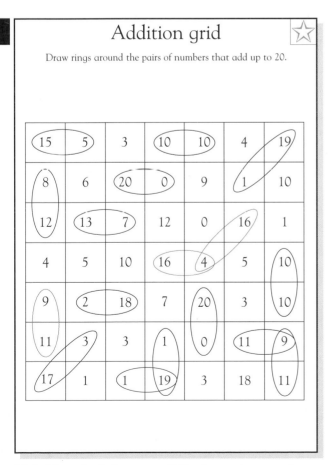

If children find this page difficult, encourage them to find 20 objects, such as counters or pennies and find different ways of separating them into 2 groups, such as 2 and 18, 15 and 5. Children can then look for these pairs of numbers.

Doubles

Write the missing numbers.

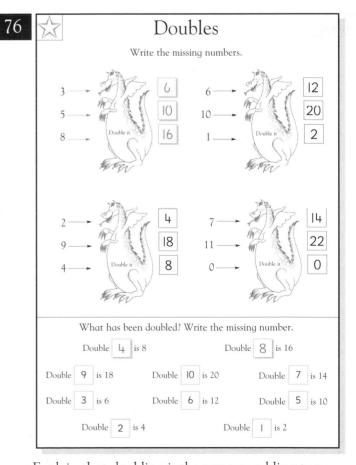

Explain that doubling is the same as adding two sets of the same number. If children cannot yet double in their heads, use counters to make two sets of the number, and add them.

Fact families

Complete each fact family.

4, 5, 9

4 + 5 = 9
5 + 4 = 9
9 − 4 = 5
9 − 5 = 4

3, 4, 7

3 + 4 = 7
4 + 3 = 7
7 − 3 = 4
7 − 4 = 3

2, 4, 6

2 + 4 = 6
4 + 2 = 6
6 − 4 = 2
6 − 2 = 4

3, 5, 8

3 + 5 = 8
5 + 3 = 8
8 − 3 = 5
8 − 5 = 3

Make sure children understand that a fact family consists of four number sentences: two are addition sentences, and two are subtraction sentences. Encourage students to see the inverse relationship between addition and subtraction with these facts.

Addition

Add to find each sum.

$$\begin{array}{r} 2\,3 \\ +\ 4 \\ \hline 27 \end{array}$$

Add to find each sum.

$$\begin{array}{r} 1\,8 \\ +\ 1 \\ \hline 19 \end{array} \qquad \begin{array}{r} 2\,3 \\ +\ 4 \\ \hline 27 \end{array} \qquad \begin{array}{r} 3\,2 \\ +\ 6 \\ \hline 38 \end{array} \qquad \begin{array}{r} 2\,0 \\ +\ 5 \\ \hline 25 \end{array}$$

$$\begin{array}{r} 3\,0 \\ +\ 9 \\ \hline 39 \end{array} \qquad \begin{array}{r} 5\,0 \\ +\ 3 \\ \hline 53 \end{array} \qquad \begin{array}{r} 1\,0 \\ +\ 4 \\ \hline 14 \end{array} \qquad \begin{array}{r} 4\,0 \\ +\ 2 \\ \hline 42 \end{array}$$

$$\begin{array}{r} 4\,2 \\ +\ 3 \\ \hline 45 \end{array} \qquad \begin{array}{r} 1\,6 \\ +\ 3 \\ \hline 19 \end{array} \qquad \begin{array}{r} 3\,4 \\ +\ 3 \\ \hline 37 \end{array} \qquad \begin{array}{r} 5\,2 \\ +\ 5 \\ \hline 57 \end{array}$$

$$\begin{array}{r} 2\,7 \\ +\ 1 \\ \hline 28 \end{array} \qquad \begin{array}{r} 1\,2 \\ +\ 4 \\ \hline 16 \end{array} \qquad \begin{array}{r} 2\,0 \\ +\ 7 \\ \hline 27 \end{array} \qquad \begin{array}{r} 1\,1 \\ +\ 7 \\ \hline 18 \end{array}$$

If children have difficulty with these exercises, make sure that they are adding in the correct order. In other words, they should add the ones first and then add the tens.

Subtraction

Subtract to find the difference.

$$\begin{array}{r} 2\,4 \\ -\ 3 \\ \hline 21 \end{array}$$

Subtract to find each difference.

$$\begin{array}{r} 1\,8 \\ -\ 1 \\ \hline 17 \end{array} \qquad \begin{array}{r} 2\,5 \\ -\ 2 \\ \hline 23 \end{array} \qquad \begin{array}{r} 3\,6 \\ -\ 2 \\ \hline 34 \end{array} \qquad \begin{array}{r} 2\,5 \\ -\ 4 \\ \hline 21 \end{array}$$

$$\begin{array}{r} 3\,9 \\ -\ 7 \\ \hline 32 \end{array} \qquad \begin{array}{r} 5\,3 \\ -\ 2 \\ \hline 51 \end{array} \qquad \begin{array}{r} 1\,4 \\ -\ 4 \\ \hline 10 \end{array} \qquad \begin{array}{r} 4\,9 \\ -\ 3 \\ \hline 46 \end{array}$$

$$\begin{array}{r} 4\,6 \\ -\ 3 \\ \hline 43 \end{array} \qquad \begin{array}{r} 1\,6 \\ -\ 5 \\ \hline 11 \end{array} \qquad \begin{array}{r} 3\,8 \\ -\ 7 \\ \hline 31 \end{array} \qquad \begin{array}{r} 5\,7 \\ -\ 5 \\ \hline 52 \end{array}$$

$$\begin{array}{r} 2\,7 \\ -\ 1 \\ \hline 26 \end{array} \qquad \begin{array}{r} 1\,4 \\ -\ 2 \\ \hline 12 \end{array} \qquad \begin{array}{r} 2\,7 \\ -\ 4 \\ \hline 23 \end{array} \qquad \begin{array}{r} 1\,7 \\ -\ 1 \\ \hline 16 \end{array}$$

Make sure children begin by subtracting the ones. If children have difficulty, point out to them that they have no tens to subtract, so they can write the tens value in the answer.

Subtraction

Subtract to find the difference.

$$\begin{array}{r} 8\,0 \\ -3\,0 \\ \hline 50 \end{array}$$

Subtract to find each difference.

$$\begin{array}{r} 3\,0 \\ -2\,0 \\ \hline 10 \end{array} \qquad \begin{array}{r} 5\,0 \\ -3\,0 \\ \hline 20 \end{array} \qquad \begin{array}{r} 4\,0 \\ -2\,0 \\ \hline 20 \end{array} \qquad \begin{array}{r} 2\,0 \\ -1\,0 \\ \hline 10 \end{array}$$

$$\begin{array}{r} 4\,0 \\ -3\,0 \\ \hline 10 \end{array} \qquad \begin{array}{r} 5\,0 \\ -2\,0 \\ \hline 30 \end{array} \qquad \begin{array}{r} 6\,0 \\ -4\,0 \\ \hline 20 \end{array} \qquad \begin{array}{r} 9\,0 \\ -3\,0 \\ \hline 60 \end{array}$$

$$\begin{array}{r} 7\,0 \\ -3\,0 \\ \hline 40 \end{array} \qquad \begin{array}{r} 9\,0 \\ -4\,0 \\ \hline 50 \end{array} \qquad \begin{array}{r} 4\,0 \\ -1\,0 \\ \hline 30 \end{array} \qquad \begin{array}{r} 5\,0 \\ -4\,0 \\ \hline 10 \end{array}$$

$$\begin{array}{r} 9\,0 \\ -7\,0 \\ \hline 20 \end{array} \qquad \begin{array}{r} 8\,0 \\ -1\,0 \\ \hline 70 \end{array} \qquad \begin{array}{r} 6\,0 \\ -5\,0 \\ \hline 10 \end{array} \qquad \begin{array}{r} 4\,0 \\ -4\,0 \\ \hline 0 \end{array}$$

Point out to children that although they are subtracting two-digit numbers, the ones digit in each number is zero, so each answer will have a zero in the ones place. Children should understand that subtracting any number from itself leaves zero.

Subtraction

Subtract to find the difference.

$$\begin{array}{r} 87 \\ -34 \\ \hline 53 \end{array}$$

Subtract to find each difference.

$\begin{array}{r} 39 \\ -27 \\ \hline 12 \end{array}$	$\begin{array}{r} 58 \\ -32 \\ \hline 26 \end{array}$	$\begin{array}{r} 44 \\ -11 \\ \hline 33 \end{array}$	$\begin{array}{r} 27 \\ -17 \\ \hline 10 \end{array}$
$\begin{array}{r} 46 \\ -33 \\ \hline 13 \end{array}$	$\begin{array}{r} 59 \\ -46 \\ \hline 13 \end{array}$	$\begin{array}{r} 75 \\ -31 \\ \hline 44 \end{array}$	$\begin{array}{r} 88 \\ -14 \\ \hline 74 \end{array}$
$\begin{array}{r} 77 \\ -33 \\ \hline 44 \end{array}$	$\begin{array}{r} 93 \\ -22 \\ \hline 71 \end{array}$	$\begin{array}{r} 67 \\ -53 \\ \hline 14 \end{array}$	$\begin{array}{r} 38 \\ -22 \\ \hline 16 \end{array}$
$\begin{array}{r} 99 \\ -79 \\ \hline 20 \end{array}$	$\begin{array}{r} 82 \\ -70 \\ \hline 12 \end{array}$	$\begin{array}{r} 69 \\ -69 \\ \hline 0 \end{array}$	$\begin{array}{r} 47 \\ -46 \\ \hline 1 \end{array}$

This page presents straightforward subtraction with two-digit numbers, with no regrouping. Make sure that children subtract in the correct order, that is, they should subtract the ones first and then the tens.

Real-life problems

All the piggy banks need 30¢. Draw different coins in each one. You can use any coin more than once.

Explain that to make 5¢, five 1¢ coins or a 5¢ coin can be used. So, 10¢ can be made with any of these combinations plus a 5¢ coin. Then another 10¢ coin will make 20¢.

Real-life problems

6¢ 5¢ 4¢ 2¢ 1¢

Draw the stamps on the letters.
You can use any stamp more than once.

6¢ 4¢ 2¢

Ms. Heather Hedgehog
1 The Leaf Pile
Snowdrop Corner
Garden City   12¢

5¢ 5¢ 5¢
5¢

Doctor Dilly Dinosaur
6 The Swamp
Mud Town   20¢

5¢ 5¢ 5¢
4¢

Rachel Robot
999 Mechanical Mansion
Metalville   24¢

6¢ 6¢ 6¢

Cheeky Charlie Chimp
100 Banana Court
Giggleton
Apeland   18¢

6¢ 5¢

Mr. Bertie Bear
The Toy Box
Betty's Bedroom
The Big House   11¢

6¢ 6¢ 6¢
1¢ 6¢

Samuel Spider
Wonder Web
Grandpa's Greenhouse
South Central Garden   25¢

Children may use different stamp combinations to reach the totals. In real-life situations, most people would use as few stamps as possible. For 6¢ postage, a 5¢ stamp and a 1¢ stamp would be better than six 1¢ stamps.

Subtraction tables

Finish each table.

−	2	3	5	10
11	9	8	6	1
15	13	12	10	5
20	18	17	15	10

−	1	6	8	9
14	13	8	6	5
19	18	13	11	10
25	24	19	17	16

−	0	4	7	11
12	12	8	5	1
28	28	24	21	17
30	30	26	23	19

Ask children to point out on the table where the information is and where the answers should go. If they need help, tell them to subtract each number in the top row from each number in the left-hand column.

Counting down

The rocket can only lift off at zero.
Use subtraction to get to 0 in 4 moves.

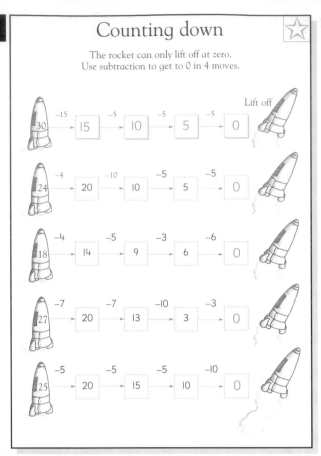

Answers will vary. If children reach zero too soon,
they can look for ways to use smaller numbers.
If they don't reach zero, they can look for larger
numbers to subtract.

Clocks

Write the times under the clocks.

4 o'clock | half past 8 | 10 o'clock
half past 5 | half past 1 | 6 o'clock

Draw the hands.

half past 7 | half past 2 | 10 o'clock
half past 11 | 3 o'clock | 9 o'clock

The lengths of the clock hands show that times
such as half past 12 and 6 o'clock are different.
Remind children that the long hand is the minute
hand and the short hand is the hour hand.

Digital clocks

Write the times under the clocks.

12:30 — half past 12 | 6:00 — 6 o'clock | 9:00 — 9 o'clock
10:30 — half past 10 | 8:30 — half past 8 | 5:00 — 5 o'clock

Fill in the digital times on the clock faces.

11:30 — half past 11 | 1:30 — half past 1 | 12:00 — 12 o'clock
3:30 — half past 3 | 8:00 — 8 o'clock | 10:00 — 10 o'clock

Watch out for confusion between the digital
versions of 5 and 2. Point out to children that the
start positions of both digital and regular numbers
are the same.

Match the times

Draw a line to connect the matching times.

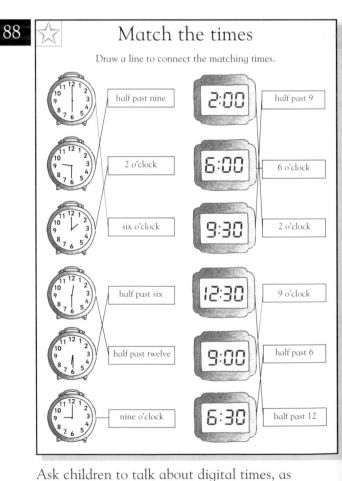

half past nine | 2:00 — half past 9
2 o'clock | 6:00 — 6 o'clock
six o'clock | 9:30 — 2 o'clock
half past six | 12:30 — 9 o'clock
half past twelve | 9:00 — half past 6
nine o'clock | 6:30 — half past 12

Ask children to talk about digital times, as
compared with times shown on analog clock
faces. Ask them which they find easier to read.

Do you know?

Put the months in order by writing a number on each page.

September **9th**   April **4th**   February **2nd**   August **8th**   May **5th**   October **10th**   March **3rd**

December **12th**   June **6th**   November **11th**   January **1st**   July **7th**

How many ...

... seconds in a minute? **60**   ... minutes in an hour? **60**

... hours in a day? **24**   ... days in a week? **7**

... days in a year? **365**   ... months in a year? **12**

Learn this rhyme.

30 days have September,
April, June, and November.
All the rest have 31,
Except February alone
That has 28 days clear
29 in each leap year.

How many days are there in your birthday month? **31**

These numbers are all facts that have to be learned rather than developed. Children can learn the rhyme and then have fun answering questions about the number of days in the month in which there is a certain holiday.

Congruent shapes

Ring the shape that matches the first shape.

Make sure children understand that two shapes can match each other exactly even if they are not oriented in the same way. Make sure they understand the difference between shapes that have straight edges and shapes that are curved.

Venn diagrams

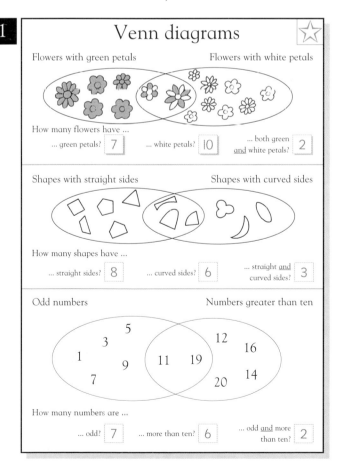

Flowers with green petals   Flowers with white petals

How many flowers have ...

... green petals? **7**   ... white petals? **10**   ... both green and white petals? **2**

Shapes with straight sides   Shapes with curved sides

How many shapes have ...

... straight sides? **8**   ... curved sides? **6**   ... straight and curved sides? **3**

Odd numbers   Numbers greater than ten

5   3   12   16   1   9   11   19   7   20   14

How many numbers are ...

... odd? **7**   ... more than ten? **6**   ... odd and more than ten? **2**

Make sure children understand that the items in the part of the diagram where the two ovals intersect are a part of both sets of items. They must be included when counting either of the main sets.

Similar shapes

Ring the shape that is the same but of a different size.

Children might need help in grasping the idea of same shape, different size. Remind children to eliminate obviously incorrect choices first.

2-dimensional shapes

Add the costs to find the cost of each picture.

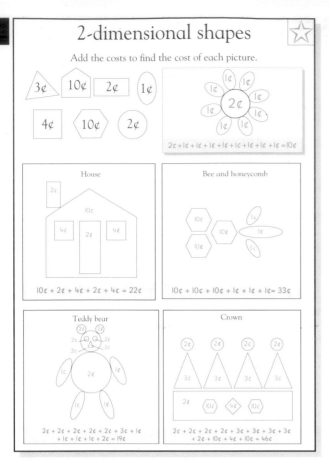

3¢   10¢   2¢   1¢

4¢   10¢   2¢

2¢

2¢ + 1¢ + 1¢ + 1¢ + 1¢ + 1¢ + 1¢ + 1¢ + 1¢ = 10¢

House
10¢ + 2¢ + 4¢ + 2¢ + 4¢ = 22¢

Bee and honeycomb
10¢ + 10¢ + 10¢ + 1¢ + 1¢ + 1¢ = 33¢

Teddy bear
2¢ + 2¢ + 2¢ + 2¢ + 2¢ + 3¢ + 1¢
+ 1¢ + 1¢ + 1¢ + 2¢ = 19¢

Crown
2¢ + 2¢ + 2¢ + 2¢ + 3¢ + 3¢ + 3¢ + 3¢
+ 2¢ + 10¢ + 4¢ + 10¢ = 46¢

Encourage children to find their own ways of
making the addition simpler. If children find
adding difficult, help them to use counters to count
out the individual amounts and then find the total.

3-dimensional shapes

Label the 3-D shapes.
(cone, cylinder, pyramid, cube, sphere, rectangular prism)

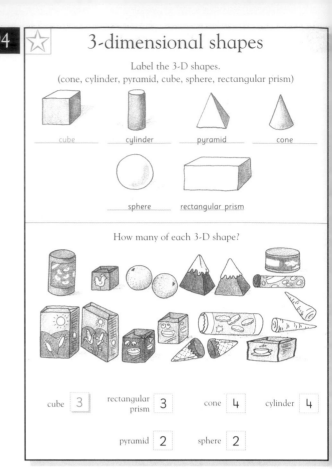

cube   cylinder   pyramid   cone

sphere   rectangular prism

How many of each 3-D shape?

cube [3]   rectangular prism [3]   cone [4]   cylinder [4]

pyramid [2]   sphere [2]

Have children describe the differences between
a cube and a prism or between a cone and a
cylinder. Children should begin to use appropriate
mathematical language such as *curved*, *straight*,
corners, *sides*, and so on.

Read, write, and draw

Write the numbers and draw the pictures.

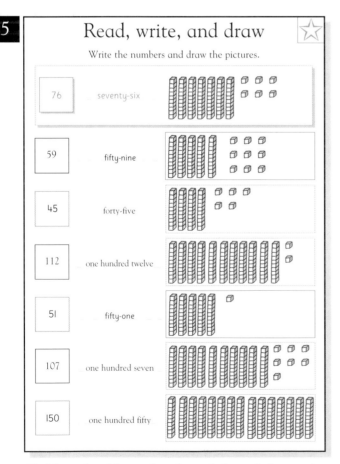

76   seventy-six

59   fifty-nine

45   forty-five

112   one hundred twelve

51   fifty-one

107   one hundred seven

150   one hundred fifty

Children should use their knowledge of place value
for this page. For example, in 107, the 1 means one
hundred, the 0 means no tens, and the 7 means
seven ones.

Counting

Count on forward or backward by 10s.
Write the missing numbers.

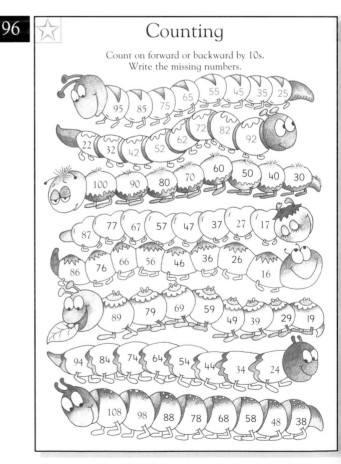

Children should determine whether the numbers
are increasing or decreasing. They can then decide
whether to count on or to count back. Children
should see that the ones digits remain unchanged
and the tens digits increase or decrease.

Bar graphs

Fruit

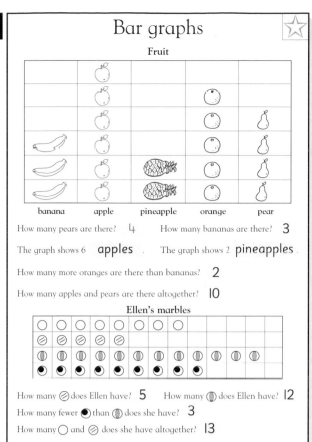

| banana | apple | pineapple | orange | pear |

How many pears are there? 4   How many bananas are there? 3

The graph shows 6 **apples** .   The graph shows 2 **pineapples** .

How many more oranges are there than bananas? 2

How many apples and pears are there altogether? 10

Ellen's marbles

How many ⊘ does Ellen have? 5   How many ◖ does Ellen have? 12

How many fewer ● than ◖ does she have? 3

How many ◯ and ⊘ does she have altogether? 13

Discuss with children what the bar graphs show, what the labels mean, and what the drawings or symbols mean. Guide children to compare the heights of the columns or the lengths of the rows to make quick comparisons of amounts.

Subtraction

If each child eats 1 slice, how many slices will be left? 5

If the children eat 6 slices, how many slices will be left? 2

If the children eat 8 slices, how many slices will be left? 0

If each child reads 1 book, how many books will be left? 8

How many books will be left if the children take 6 books altogether? 6

How many books will be left if the children take 9 books? 3

If the dog buries 1 ball, how many balls are left? 6

Write a subtraction sentence. $7 - 1 = 6$

If the dog buries 3 balls, how many balls are left? 4

Write a subtraction sentence. $7 - 3 = 4$

Guide children to see that when they take something away from a set of things or a whole, something is left behind. What is left behind is less than or smaller than what was there originally. This procedure is called subtraction.

2s, 5s, and 10s

Count by 2s, 5s and 10s to help you connect the dots.

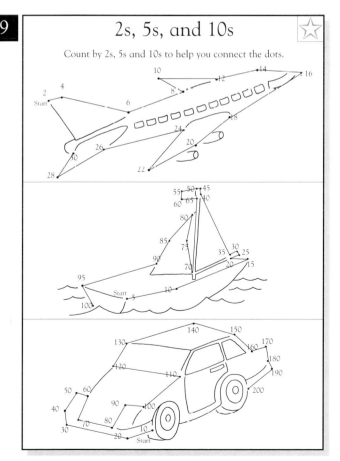

Make sure that children understand the patterns in the number sequences. Have them practice counting by 2s, 5s, and 10s before connecting the dots.

Comparing

Complete the boxes.

2 less	number	2 more
51	53	55

number	between	number
96	97 98	99

number	between	number
20	21 22 23	24

3 less	number	3 more
27	30	33

2 less	number	2 more
27	29	31

number	between	number
18	19 20 21	22

number	between	number
131	132 133	134

10 less	number	10 more
109	119	129

5 less	number	5 more
80	85	90

number	between	number
40	41 42 43 44	45

number	between	number
99	100 101	102

5 less	number	5 more
151	156	161

Make sure children understand the meaning of *more*, *less*, and *between*. Have them give examples such as 3 more or 3 less than 10. Children should see that they must fill in the sequence of numbers that lie between two numbers.

Ordering

Find the totals.

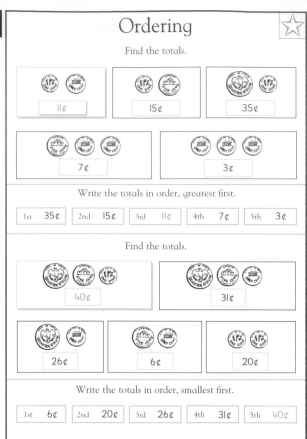

11¢   15¢   35¢

7¢   3¢

Write the totals in order, greatest first.

| 1st | 35¢ | 2nd | 15¢ | 3rd | 11¢ | 4th | 7¢ | 5th | 3¢ |

Find the totals.

40¢   31¢

26¢   6¢   20¢

Write the totals in order, smallest first.

| 1st | 6¢ | 2nd | 20¢ | 3rd | 26¢ | 4th | 31¢ | 5th | 40¢ |

Have children practice writing amounts of money, using the symbol for cents (¢). Discuss strategies for adding money, such as adding the coins of greater value first.

Subtraction

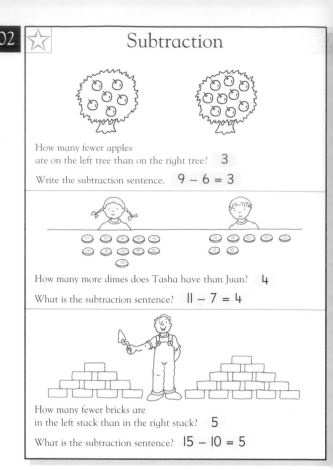

How many fewer apples
are on the left tree than on the right tree?   3

Write the subtraction sentence.   9 − 6 = 3

How many more dimes does Tasha have than Juan?   4

What is the subtraction sentence?   11 − 7 = 4

How many fewer bricks are
in the left stack than in the right stack?   5

What is the subtraction sentence?   15 − 10 = 5

Guide children to understand that they can use subtraction to compare quantities. By subtracting, children can find out how much more or how much less or how many more or how many fewer one quantity is than another.

Matching fractions

Color the matching squares.

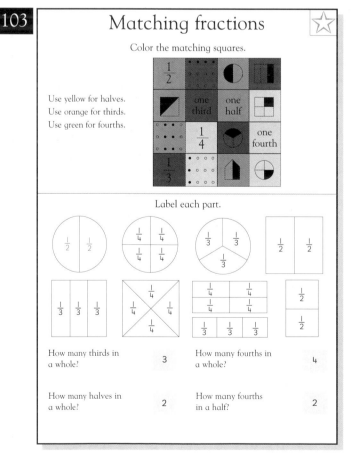

Use yellow for halves.
Use orange for thirds.
Use green for fourths.

Label each part.

How many thirds in
a whole?   3

How many fourths in
a whole?   4

How many halves in
a whole?   2

How many fourths
in a half?   2

Children can look back at the drawings they labeled for help in answering the questions in the last section on the page.

Money

You have only 3 coins in each purse. Draw the 3 coins that make the exact amount needed. You may use each coin more than once.

Limiting the number of coins causes children to think more carefully about which coins they should use. Children may need help realizing that it would help to begin with the largest coin.

Fact families

Use the 3 numbers to write 4 different facts.

6 + 7 = 13	7 + 6 = 13	13 – 7 = 6	13 – 6 = 7
16 + 4 = 20	4 + 16 = 20	20 – 4 = 16	20 – 16 = 4
6 + 5 = 11	5 + 6 = 11	11 – 5 = 6	11 – 6 = 5
7 + 8 = 15	8 + 7 = 15	15 – 7 = 8	15 – 8 = 7
8 + 12 = 20	12 + 8 = 20	20 – 8 = 12	20 – 12 = 8
10 + 8 = 18	8 + 10 = 18	18 – 10 = 8	18 – 8 = 10
8 + 9 = 17	9 + 8 = 17	17 – 9 = 8	17 – 8 = 9
9 + 7 = 16	7 + 9 = 16	16 – 9 = 7	16 – 7 = 9
14 + 6 = 20	6 + 14 = 20	20 – 14 = 6	20 – 6 = 14
11 + 8 = 19	8 + 11 = 19	19 – 11 = 8	19 – 8 = 11

Help children to understand that if they know one
addition fact, they can form three other facts: one
more addition fact and two subtraction facts.
For example, 6 + 7 = 13 allows the formation of
7 + 6 = 13, 13 – 6 = 7, and 13 – 7 = 6.

Adding money

Add the money. Write the totals in the right squares.

+	2¢	5¢	8¢	6¢
3¢	5¢	8¢	11¢	9¢
11¢	13¢	16¢	19¢	17¢
29¢	31¢	34¢	37¢	35¢
32¢	34¢	37¢	40¢	38¢

+	2¢	4¢	6¢	9¢	3¢
17¢	19¢	21¢	23¢	26¢	20¢
20¢	22¢	24¢	26¢	29¢	23¢
33¢	35¢	37¢	39¢	42¢	36¢
41¢	43¢	45¢	47¢	50¢	44¢

Have children practice writing amounts of money,
using the symbol for cents (¢). Discuss strategies for
adding money, such as adding the coins of greater
value first.

Using doubles

Use the doubles to find the answers.

6 + 6 = 12	10 + 10 = 20
6 + 7 6 + 6 + 1 = 13	10 + 11 10 + 10 + 1 = 21
6 + 5 6 + 6 – 1 = 11	10 + 9 10 + 10 – 1 = 19

Use doubles to find the answers.

4 + 4 = 8   4 + 5 = 4 + 4 + 1 = 9

4 + 3 = 4 + 4 – 1 = 7

7 + 7 = 14   7 + 8 = 7 + 7 + 1 = 15

7 + 6 = 7 + 7 – 1 = 13

8 + 8 = 16   8 + 9 = 8 + 8 + 1 = 17

8 + 7 = 8 + 8 – 1 = 15

Double your doubles.

1 double it 2 double it 4   4 double it 8 double it 16

2 double it 4 double it 8   5 double it 10 double it 20

3 double it 6 double it 12   6 double it 12 double it 24

Guide children to see that doubles, doubles plus 1,
and doubles minus 1 can be useful strategies for
solving addition problems.

Adding up

Add the numbers on the sails. Write the totals on the boats.

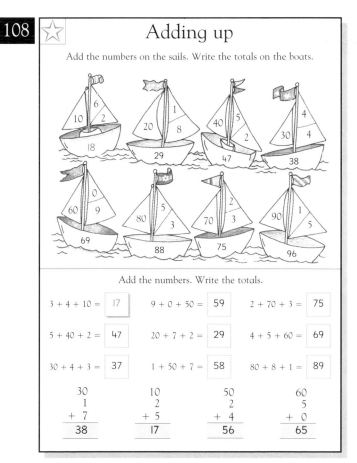

Add the numbers. Write the totals.

3 + 4 + 10 = 17   9 + 0 + 50 = 59   2 + 70 + 3 = 75

5 + 40 + 2 = 47   20 + 7 + 2 = 29   4 + 5 + 60 = 69

30 + 4 + 3 = 37   1 + 50 + 7 = 58   80 + 8 + 1 = 89

```
  30        10        50        60
   1         2         2         5
 + 7       + 5       + 4       + 0
 ----      ----      ----      ----
  38        17        56        65
```

Help children to identify ways to make the addition
problems simpler. Children can use what they know
about addition facts and about adding 10s.

Count by 2s

Draw the pictures. Count by 2s. Write the totals.

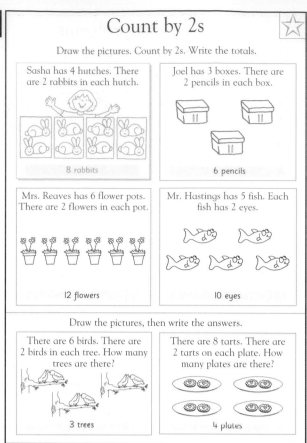

Sasha has 4 hutches. There are 2 rabbits in each hutch.

8 rabbits

Joel has 3 boxes. There are 2 pencils in each box.

6 pencils

Mrs. Reaves has 6 flower pots. There are 2 flowers in each pot.

12 flowers

Mr. Hastings has 5 fish. Each fish has 2 eyes.

10 eyes

Draw the pictures, then write the answers.

There are 6 birds. There are 2 birds in each tree. How many trees are there?

3 trees

There are 8 tarts. There are 2 tarts on each plate. How many plates are there?

4 plates

Children should by now be comfortable with this counting sequence. For the last two exercises, help them to find the number of groups of 2 that make up the greater number.

Addition

Add to find each sum.

$$\begin{array}{r} 42 \\ +13 \\ \hline 55 \end{array} \qquad \begin{array}{r} 84 \\ +10 \\ \hline 94 \end{array} \qquad \begin{array}{r} 18 \\ +21 \\ \hline 39 \end{array}$$

Add to find each sum.

$$\begin{array}{r} 15 \\ +34 \\ \hline 49 \end{array} \qquad \begin{array}{r} 68 \\ +21 \\ \hline 89 \end{array} \qquad \begin{array}{r} 33 \\ +11 \\ \hline 44 \end{array} \qquad \begin{array}{r} 32 \\ +43 \\ \hline 75 \end{array}$$

$$\begin{array}{r} 54 \\ +12 \\ \hline 66 \end{array} \qquad \begin{array}{r} 27 \\ +21 \\ \hline 48 \end{array} \qquad \begin{array}{r} 35 \\ +52 \\ \hline 87 \end{array} \qquad \begin{array}{r} 11 \\ +11 \\ \hline 22 \end{array}$$

$$\begin{array}{r} 72 \\ +23 \\ \hline 95 \end{array} \qquad \begin{array}{r} 15 \\ +53 \\ \hline 68 \end{array} \qquad \begin{array}{r} 10 \\ +19 \\ \hline 29 \end{array} \qquad \begin{array}{r} 86 \\ +11 \\ \hline 97 \end{array}$$

$$\begin{array}{r} 13 \\ +42 \\ \hline 55 \end{array} \qquad \begin{array}{r} 36 \\ +32 \\ \hline 68 \end{array} \qquad \begin{array}{r} 70 \\ +14 \\ \hline 84 \end{array} \qquad \begin{array}{r} 64 \\ +25 \\ \hline 89 \end{array}$$

$$\begin{array}{r} 21 \\ +53 \\ \hline 74 \end{array} \qquad \begin{array}{r} 42 \\ +41 \\ \hline 83 \end{array} \qquad \begin{array}{r} 18 \\ +11 \\ \hline 29 \end{array} \qquad \begin{array}{r} 16 \\ +20 \\ \hline 36 \end{array}$$

This page presents straightforward addition of two-digit numbers, with no regrouping. Make sure that children add in the correct order, that is, they should add the ones first and then add the tens.

Addition

Add to find each sum.

$$\begin{array}{r} 65 \\ +31 \\ \hline 96 \end{array} \qquad \begin{array}{r} 14 \\ +24 \\ \hline 38 \end{array} \qquad \begin{array}{r} 50 \\ +10 \\ \hline 60 \end{array}$$

Add to find each sum.

$$\begin{array}{r} 24 \\ +24 \\ \hline 48 \end{array} \qquad \begin{array}{r} 57 \\ +11 \\ \hline 68 \end{array} \qquad \begin{array}{r} 30 \\ +45 \\ \hline 75 \end{array} \qquad \begin{array}{r} 17 \\ +32 \\ \hline 49 \end{array}$$

$$\begin{array}{r} 64 \\ +22 \\ \hline 86 \end{array} \qquad \begin{array}{r} 15 \\ +13 \\ \hline 28 \end{array} \qquad \begin{array}{r} 52 \\ +21 \\ \hline 73 \end{array} \qquad \begin{array}{r} 55 \\ +40 \\ \hline 95 \end{array}$$

$$\begin{array}{r} 16 \\ +33 \\ \hline 49 \end{array} \qquad \begin{array}{r} 29 \\ +20 \\ \hline 49 \end{array} \qquad \begin{array}{r} 61 \\ +35 \\ \hline 96 \end{array} \qquad \begin{array}{r} 74 \\ +12 \\ \hline 86 \end{array}$$

Michael has 21 fish. His dad gives him 11 more fish. How many fish does Michael have?

32

$$\begin{array}{r} 21 \\ +11 \\ \hline 32 \end{array}$$

Sonia read 13 books one month. She read 15 books the next month. How many books did she read in all?

28

$$\begin{array}{r} 13 \\ +15 \\ \hline 28 \end{array}$$

This page also presents straightforward addition of two-digit numbers, with no regrouping. Once again, make sure that children add the ones first and then the tens.

Addition and subtraction

Write the missing numbers.

$$? + 8 = 12 \qquad 7 - ? = 1$$
$$4 + 8 = 12 \qquad 7 - 6 = 1$$

Write the missing numbers.

15 − **5** = 10	3 + **3** = 6	8 − **6** = 2
9 + **2** = 11	8 − **8** = 0	9 + **5** = 14
7 + **3** = 10	6 − **4** = 2	17 − **10** = 7
5 − **4** = 1	2 + **5** = 7	1 + **3** = 4
14 − **7** = 7	8 + **1** = 9	3 + **9** = 12
8 + **6** = 14	3 − **1** = 2	12 − **6** = 6
18 − **9** = 9	5 + **6** = 11	1 − **1** = 0
11 − **7** = 4	4 + **9** = 13	3 + **5** = 8
2 + **3** = 5	16 − **6** = 10	8 + **10** = 18
5 + **7** = 12	4 + **4** = 0	9 − **3** = 6

Children should use their knowledge of fact families to solve the problems on this page. If they need help, remind them that fact families are made up of two addition facts and two subtraction facts.

Real-life problems

Look at the picture. Answer the questions.

What time is it ? __4:30__

Today is Friday. What day was it yesterday? __Thursday__

How many cupcakes can each person have? __two__

If half of the apples were eaten, how many would be left? __three__

If each person had 2 drinks, how many drinks would there be altogether? __eight__

How many more sandwiches are there than apples? __four__

If 13 candies were eaten, how many would be left? __seven__

Each package contains 2 presents. How many presents are there altogether? __six__

What shape are the sandwiches? __triangular__

Is there an odd or an even number of chairs? __even__

Children have to decide what each question is asking for and then find a way of arriving at each answer. For example, they recognize that the fifth question can be answered by counting by 2s.

Real-life problems

Complete the pictures, and then write the answers.

There were 12 biscuits. James ate 3. How many were left?

__9__

Share 12 marbles equally among 3 people. How many marbles will each have?

__4__

Susie has ten fish. She is given 11 more for her birthday. How many fish does she have altogether?

__21__

Joe had 5 boxes. He had 3 pencils in each box. How many pencils did he have altogether?

__15__

If you share 16 carrots equally among 4 rabbits, how many carrots will each have?

__4__

Mom had 16 cups, but she broke 9 of them. How many cups does she have left?

__7__

Children have to decide which operation to use and what kind of answer each question calls for. Call their attention to the words *altogether* and *left*. Point out that these words are clues whether to add or subtract.

Addition

Find each sum.

$$\begin{array}{r} 40 \\ +30 \\ \hline 70 \end{array} \qquad \begin{array}{r} 80 \\ +80 \\ \hline 160 \end{array} \qquad \begin{array}{r} 20 \\ +50 \\ \hline 70 \end{array} \qquad \begin{array}{r} 90 \\ +30 \\ \hline 120 \end{array}$$

$$\begin{array}{r} 10 \\ +10 \\ \hline 20 \end{array} \qquad \begin{array}{r} 70 \\ +50 \\ \hline 120 \end{array} \qquad \begin{array}{r} 80 \\ +40 \\ \hline 120 \end{array} \qquad \begin{array}{r} 50 \\ +30 \\ \hline 80 \end{array}$$

$$\begin{array}{r} 60 \\ +80 \\ \hline 140 \end{array} \qquad \begin{array}{r} 50 \\ +50 \\ \hline 100 \end{array} \qquad \begin{array}{r} 20 \\ +10 \\ \hline 30 \end{array} \qquad \begin{array}{r} 30 \\ +120 \\ \hline 50 \end{array}$$

$$\begin{array}{r} 40 \\ +70 \\ \hline 110 \end{array} \qquad \begin{array}{r} 20 \\ +40 \\ \hline 60 \end{array} \qquad \begin{array}{r} 90 \\ +40 \\ \hline 130 \end{array} \qquad \begin{array}{r} 10 \\ +30 \\ \hline 40 \end{array}$$

Find each sum.

70 + 20 = 90   80 + 70 = 150   10 + 40 = 50

60 + 60 = 120   30 + 30 = 60   50 + 100 = 150

20 + 70 = 90   70 + 90 = 160   10 + 20 = 30

90 + 60 = 150   40 + 40 = 80   80 + 10 = 90

Point out to children that even though they are adding two-digit numbers, they can write a zero in the ones place in each answer, because they are adding 10s.

Clocks and watches

Write the times.

4 o'clock

half past 10

9 o'clock

half past 5

11 o'clock

half past 2

half past 1

12 o'clock

half past 7

10 o'clock

half past 3

Encourage children to express times both as digital numbers and on analog clock faces.

Puzzles

Read the clues and solve the puzzle.

I am a number between 20 and 30. If you
count by fives, you will say my name. Who am I? 25

Read the clues and solve each puzzle.

I am an even number. I am between 6 and 9. Who am I? 8

7 + 7 is less than I am. 7 + 9 is greater than I am. Who am I? 15

I am a number less than 10. If you add me to
myself, you will find a number greater than 16. Who am I? 9

16 – 10 is less than I am. 16 – 8 is greater than I am. Who am I? 7

I am a number between 7 and 12. If you
count by threes, you will say my name. Who am I? 9

I am an odd number. I am between 41 and 44. Who am I? 43

If you subtract me from 14, you will find a
number greater than 11. I am an odd number. Who am I? 1

If you add me to 50, you will find a number less than 70.
If you count by tens you will say my name. Who am I? 10

If you add me to 1, you will find
an odd number. I am less than 2. Who am I? 0

Encourage children to use their knowledge of
counting sequences, and addition and subtraction
facts to solve the puzzles. If necessary, read the
clues together.

Tables

Water animals

	Has 4 legs	Eats insects	Has a furry coat	Lays eggs
Frog	yes	yes	no	yes
Newt	yes	yes	no	yes
Otter	yes	no	yes	no

Use the table to answer the questions.

What does the   insects   Who lays eggs?   frog, newt
frog eat?

Who has a furry coat? otter   Does the otter   no
                                        eat insects?

Who has a furry coat and does not lay eggs?   otter

School friends

	Age	Hobby	Pet	Favorite color
Dean	7	Computers	Rat	Black
Joe	6	Reading	Rabbit	Purple
Taif	7	Judo	Cat	Orange
Maddie	8	Computers	Parrot	Green

Use the table to answer the questions.

Whose favorite
color is black? Dean's   Who is the oldest? Maddie

Who has judo   What kind of pet
for a hobby? Taif   does Joe have? rabbit

Who likes computers   Who is seven and
and has a parrot? Maddie   does not have a rat? Taif

Guide children to see that the first column in the
table on top lists the animals and the next four
columns describe them. Help them to see that
the second table is the same but describes friends.

Venn diagrams

Things made with metal   Things made with plastic

How many things are ...?

made with plastic? 6   made with metal? 7

made with metal and plastic? 3   not made with plastic? 4

Odd numbers   Numbers greater than 20

3 15   24 26
1   21 25   30
7 19   22

How many numbers are ...?

odd? 7   greater than 20? 6

odd and greater than 20? 2   not odd? 4

White things   Green things

How many things are ...?

green? 5   white? 6

green and white? 2   not green? 4

Make sure children understand that the items
in the part of the diagram where the two ovals
intersect are a part of both sets of items. They
must be included when counting either of
the main sets.

Appropriate units of measure

Which unit would you use to measure the
length of each item? Circle the answer.

	(inches)	miles	pounds	quarts
	miles	ounces	pounds	(yards)

Which unit would you use to measure the
weight of each item? Circle the answer.

	inches	miles	pounds	(ounces)
	miles	(pounds)	quarts	ounces

Which unit would you use to measure how much liquid
each container holds? Circle the answer.

	tons	inches	(pints)	pounds
	miles	inches	ounces	(gallons)

Discuss with children the relative magnitudes of
various units of measure. Lead them to see that
smaller units of measure should be used for smaller
items, and larger units for larger items.

Symmetry

Draw a line of symmetry on each picture.

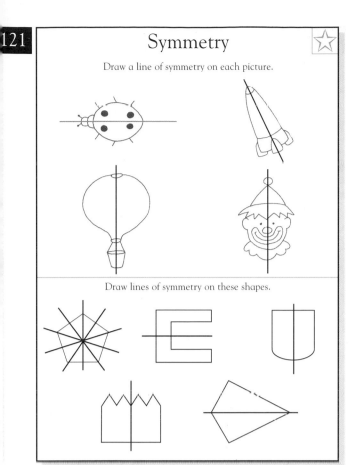

Draw lines of symmetry on these shapes.

Explain to children that a line of symmetry separates something into two halves that are mirror images of each other. If children have difficulty, suggest that they look at the items from different angles.

2-dimensional shapes

Write the name of the shape. Count the corners and sides.

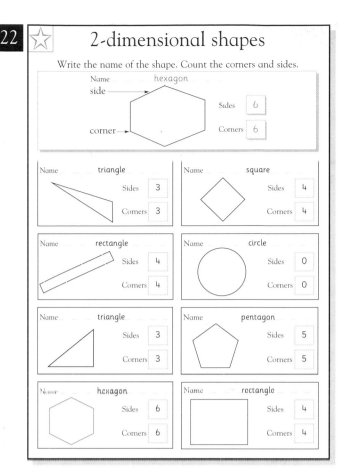

The second figure, although partially rotated, is still a square, not a diamond. Children should be able to identify the shapes by counting the number of sides and corners of each shape.

Equal value

Circle the coins that add up to the amount shown.

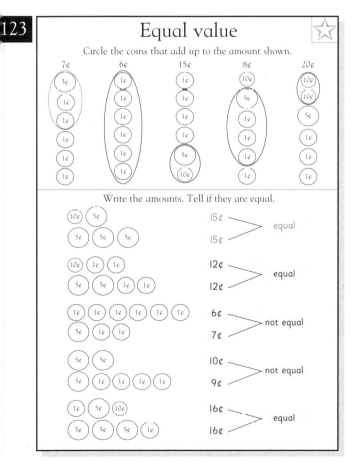

Write the amounts. Tell if they are equal.

Encourage children to begin with the largest coin possible when they are deciding which coins to use to make the desired amount.

Shapes and places

Look at the shapes and answer the questions.

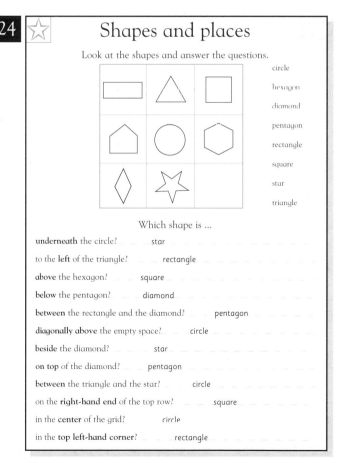

Which shape is ...

underneath the circle?   star

to the left of the triangle?   rectangle

above the hexagon?   square

below the pentagon?   diamond

between the rectangle and the diamond?   pentagon

diagonally above the empty space?   circle

beside the diamond?   star

on top of the diamond?   pentagon

between the triangle and the star?   circle

on the right-hand end of the top row?   square

in the center of the grid?   circle

in the top left-hand corner?   rectangle

This page gives children practice with words that specify position or location. Help them with the questions, if necessary.

Numbers

Which numbers are the snakes hiding?

(Hundred grid puzzle with snakes covering various numbers. Visible grid numbers include rows 1–100 with several cells hidden by snakes. Additional number tiles: 6 / 16 17 / 10 20 / 29 30 / 37 / 75 / 85 86 87 / 97 / 32 33 34 / 89 90 / 14 / 42 43 44 / 99 100 / 25 / 51 / 46 / 62 / 56 / 83 / 71 72 / 66 67 68 / 91 92 / 94)

Ask children to explain how they can tell which numbers are hidden. Encourage them to use their knowledge of counting sequences, 5s and 10s and to look at both columns and rows.

Counting by 1s, 10s, and 100s

Finish each row.

Count by 1s.	24	25	26	27	28	29
Count by 10s.	31	41	51	61	71	81
Count by 100s.	134	234	334	434	534	634

Finish each row. Count by 1s.

17	18	19	20	21	22	23	24
36	37	38	39	40	41	42	43
69	70	71	72	73	74	75	76
45	46	47	48	49	50	51	52
85	86	87	88	89	90	91	92

Finish each row. Count by 10s.

34	44	54	64	74	84	94	104
47	57	67	77	87	97	107	117
78	88	98	108	118	128	138	148
9	19	29	39	49	59	69	79
167	177	187	197	207	217	227	237
305	315	325	335	345	355	365	375

Finish each row. Count by 100s.

146	246	346	446	546	646	746	846
312	412	512	612	712	812	912	1012
508	608	708	808	908	1008	1108	1208
757	857	957	1057	1157	1257	1357	1457
274	374	474	574	674	774	874	974

Children should realize that they need only increase the digit in the appropriate place value by 1. If they have difficulty with numbers such as 96 or 957, show them that the appropriate digit increases by 1, just as in counting by 1s.

Counting by 2s

| Count by 2s. | 12 | 14 | 16 | 18 | 20 | 22 |
| Count by 2s. | 31 | 33 | 35 | 37 | 39 | 41 |

Finish each row. Count by 2s.

17	19	21	23	25	27	29	31
36	38	40	42	44	46	48	50
72	74	76	78	80	82	84	86
43	45	47	49	51	53	55	57
14	16	18	20	22	24	26	28
39	41	43	45	47	49	51	53

Finish each row. Count by 2s.

20	22	24	26	28	30	32	34
75	77	79	81	83	85	87	89
44	46	48	50	52	54	56	58
69	71	73	75	77	79	81	83
31	33	35	37	39	41	43	45
88	90	92	94	96	98	100	102

Finish each row. Count by 2s.

20	22	24	26	28	30	32	34
47	49	51	53	55	57	59	61
77	79	81	83	85	87	89	91
46	48	50	52	54	56	58	60
87	89	91	93	95	97	99	101
46	48	50	52	54	56	58	60

As on the previous page, some children will need help crossing a tens or hundreds "border." Show them counting by 2s by counting by 1 two times.

Odd and even

| Numbers ending in | 0 | 2 | 4 | 6 | 8 | are called even numbers. |
| Numbers ending in | 1 | 3 | 5 | 7 | 9 | are called odd numbers. |

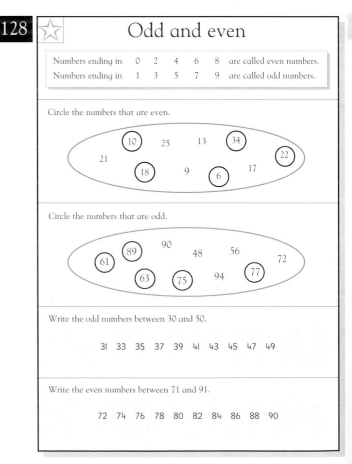

Circle the numbers that are even.

(10) 25 13 (34) 21 (18) 9 (6) 17 (22)

Circle the numbers that are odd.

(89) 90 48 56 72 (61) (63) (75) 94 (77)

Write the odd numbers between 30 and 50.

31 33 35 37 39 41 43 45 47 49

Write the even numbers between 71 and 91.

72 74 76 78 80 82 84 86 88 90

Children should realize that even numbers are all multiples of 2 and that all even numbers can be divided by 2 and give a whole-number quotient. Odd numbers cannot be divided by 2. If they are unsure, let them use counters and try to share them equally.

More and less

Which number is 1 more than 49?	50
Which number is 10 less than 764?	754
Which number is 100 less than 187?	87

Write the number that is 1 more than each of these.

| 35 | 36 | 78 | 79 | 69 | 70 | 53 | 54 | 9 | 10 | 654 | 655 |
| 41 | 42 | 124 | 125 | 167 | 168 | 40 | 41 | | | 236 | 237 | 473 | 474 |

Write the number that is 1 less than each of these.

| 52 | 51 | 18 | 17 | 20 | 19 | 76 | 75 | 37 | 36 | 150 | 149 |
| 50 | 49 | 154 | 153 | 423 | 422 | 100 | 99 | 531 | 530 | 483 | 482 |

Write the number that is 10 more than each of these.

46	56	21	31	86	96	153	163	216	226
185	195	298	308	399	409	538	548	490	500
601	611	990	1000	590	600	323	333	480	490

Write the number that is 10 less than each of these.

56	46	75	65	86	76	185	175	230	220
680	670	451	441	503	493	407	397	805	795
600	590	902	892	605	595	702	692	908	898

Write the number that is 100 more than each of these.

| 365 | 465 | 76 | 176 |
| 960 | 1060 | 601 | 701 |

Write the number that is 100 less than each of these.

| 502 | 402 | 100 | 0 |
| 809 | 709 | 750 | 650 |

Children may be uncertain when addition or subtraction takes them over a tens or hundreds "border," for example, where the child is asked to write 10 more than 298.

Fact families

Finish the fact family for each group of numbers.

9		5 + 4 = 9
5	4	4 + 5 = 9
		9 − 4 = 5
		9 − 5 = 4

Finish the fact family for each group of numbers.

7		8		7		6
4	3	3	5	6	1	2	4
4 + 3 = 7	3 + 5 = 8	6 + 1 = 7	2 + 4 = 6
3 + 4 = 7	5 + 3 = 8	1 + 6 = 7	4 + 2 = 6
7 − 3 = 4	8 − 5 = 3	7 − 1 = 6	6 − 4 = 2
7 − 4 = 3	8 − 3 = 5	7 − 6 = 1	6 − 2 = 4

9		5		3		8
2	7	2	5	1	4	10	2
2 + 7 = 9	3 + 2 = 5	3 + 1 = 4	2 + 8 = 10
7 + 2 = 9	2 + 3 = 5	1 + 3 = 4	8 + 2 = 10
9 − 2 = 7	5 − 2 = 3	4 − 1 = 3	10 − 2 = 8
9 − 7 = 2	5 − 3 = 2	4 − 3 = 1	10 − 8 = 2

10	5	4	8	3	6	4	2
5 + 5 = 10	4 + 4 = 8	3 + 3 = 6	2 + 2 = 4
10 − 5 = 5	8 − 4 = 4	6 − 3 = 3	4 − 2 = 2

Write the fact family for each group of numbers.

10	3	7	3	9	6	6	8	2	5	7	2
7 + 3 = 10	3 + 6 = 9	6 + 2 = 8	5 + 2 = 7
3 + 7 = 10	6 + 3 = 9	2 + 6 = 8	2 + 5 = 7
10 − 3 = 7	9 − 3 = 6	8 − 2 = 6	7 − 2 = 5
10 − 7 = 3	9 − 6 = 3	8 − 6 = 2	7 − 5 = 2

Children should understand that subtraction "undoes" addition. You may want to use counters to show the addition fact families.

Fractions

Color one-third ($\frac{1}{3}$) of each shape.

Color one-half ($\frac{1}{2}$) of each shape.

Color one-fourth ($\frac{1}{4}$) of each shape.

Color one-third ($\frac{1}{3}$) of each shape.

Color one-eighth ($\frac{1}{8}$) of each shape.

Color one-tenth ($\frac{1}{10}$) of each shape.

Sections other than those shown above may be colored, but children must only color one section in each shape. It is important for them to realize that the bottom number represents how many parts the whole has been divided into.

Adding

Write the answers between the lines.

35	17	24
+16	+ 9	+ 8
51	26	32

Write the answers between the lines.

24	43	21	46
+ 9	+ 6	+ 7	+ 5
33	49	28	51

43	72	64	38
+ 7	+ 5	+ 7	+ 8
50	77	71	46

46	37	53	49
+10	+11	+12	+ 9
56	48	65	58

Write the answers between the lines.

9	8	7	8
7	9	9	8
+ 9	+ 7	+ 6	+ 9
25	24	22	25

12¢	18¢	8¢	13¢
6¢	7¢	11¢	9¢
+10¢	+10¢	+ 6¢	+ 6¢
28¢	35¢	25¢	28¢

20¢	15¢	8¢	10¢
7¢	10¢	10¢	8¢
+10¢	+ 2¢	+ 4¢	+10¢
37¢	27¢	22¢	28¢

For many of these exercises, make sure that children do not neglect to regroup. For the final two rows of the second section, children should add all of the ones column first.

Estimating length

Circle the longest string.

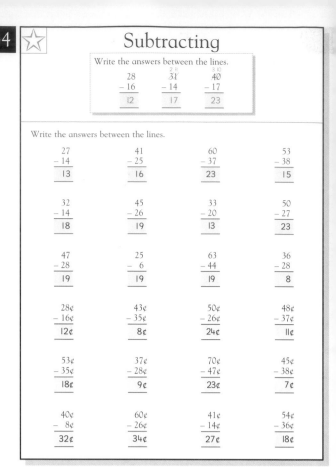

Circle the shortest string.

Circle the longest string.

Look at the ruler. Circle the closest measure.

1 inch   2 inches   (3 inches)   4 inches

2 inches   3 inches   (4 inches)   6 inches

2 inches   3 inches   4 inches   (6 inches)

Children should be able to compare the lengths by sight. For the last section of the page, allow them to use a benchmark (such as the length of one joint of a finger) to estimate length.

Subtracting

Write the answers between the lines.

28	2 11 31	3 10 40
− 16	− 14	− 17
12	17	23

Write the answers between the lines.

27	41	60	53
− 14	− 25	− 37	− 38
13	16	23	15

32	45	33	50
− 14	− 26	− 20	− 27
18	19	13	23

47	25	63	36
− 28	− 6	− 44	− 28
19	19	19	8

28¢	43¢	50¢	48¢
− 16¢	− 35¢	− 26¢	− 37¢
12¢	8¢	24¢	11¢

53¢	37¢	70¢	45¢
− 35¢	− 28¢	− 47¢	− 38¢
18¢	9¢	23¢	7¢

40¢	60¢	41¢	54¢
− 8¢	− 26¢	− 14¢	− 36¢
32¢	34¢	27¢	18¢

In some of these exercises, children may incorrectly subtract the larger digit from the smaller one, when they should be subtracting the smaller digit from the larger one. In such cases, point out that children should regroup.

Simple tally charts and bar graphs

Look at the tally chart and then answer the question.

| blue | ⦀⦀ ⦀⦀ ⦀⦀ ⦀⦀⦀ | How many votes did blue receive? | 18 |
| red | ⦀⦀ ⦀⦀ | | |

Look at the tally chart and then answer the questions.

Favorite ice cream flavors

vanilla	⦀⦀ ⦀⦀ ⦀
chocolate	⦀⦀ ⦀⦀ ⦀⦀ ⦀⦀ ⦀⦀⦀⦀
strawberry	⦀⦀ ⦀⦀ ⦀⦀ ⦀⦀⦀

Which flavor had the most votes?   chocolate

Which flavor had 11 votes?   vanilla

What was the difference in votes between the most popular flavor and strawberry?   6

Look at the bar graph and then answer the questions.

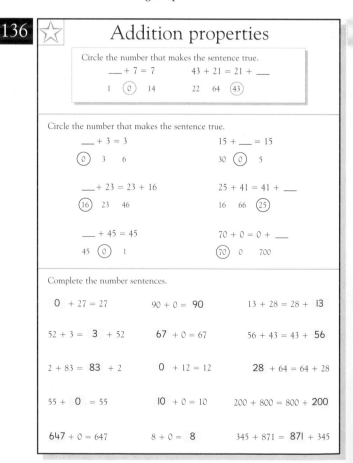

Favorite sports

Number of votes — football, volleyball, hockey, running

Which sport did four children vote for?   football

How many votes did volleyball receive?   5

Which was the least popular sport?   running

How many children voted altogether?   13

How many more voted for football than for hockey?   1

Children usually accept the concept of tally marks very quickly. They can count on by 5s for completed tallies.

Addition properties

Circle the number that makes the sentence true.

___ + 7 = 7   43 + 21 = 21 + ___

1   (0)   14   22   64   (43)

Circle the number that makes the sentence true.

___ + 3 = 3   15 + ___ = 15

(0)   3   6   30   (0)   5

___ + 23 = 23 + 16   25 + 41 = 41 + ___

(16)   23   46   16   66   (25)

___ + 45 = 45   70 + 0 = 0 + ___

45   (0)   1   (70)   0   700

Complete the number sentences.

0 + 27 = 27   90 + 0 = 90   13 + 28 = 28 + 13

52 + 3 = 3 + 52   67 + 0 = 67   56 + 43 = 43 + 56

2 + 83 = 83 + 2   0 + 12 = 12   28 + 64 = 64 + 28

55 + 0 = 55   10 + 0 = 10   200 + 800 = 800 + 200

647 + 0 = 647   8 + 0 = 8   345 + 871 = 871 + 345

This page tests children's understanding of the zero property and the commutative property of addition. Make sure that they understand that the order of addends does not affect the answer.

Equations

Circle the correct number sentence.

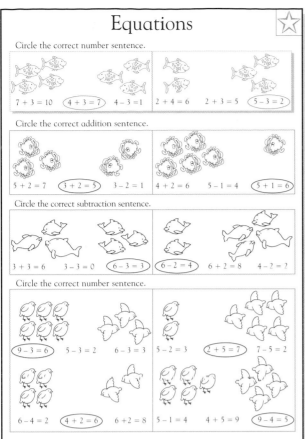

7 + 3 = 10   (4 + 3 = 7)   4 – 3 = 1   2 + 4 = 6   2 + 3 = 5   (5 – 3 = 2)

Circle the correct addition sentence.

5 + 2 = 7   (3 + 2 = 5)   3 – 2 = 1   4 + 2 = 6   5 – 1 = 4   (5 + 1 = 6)

Circle the correct subtraction sentence.

3 + 3 = 6   3 – 3 = 0   (6 – 3 = 3)   (6 – 2 = 4)   6 + 2 = 8   4 – 2 = 2

Circle the correct number sentence.

(9 – 3 = 6)   5 – 3 = 2   6 – 3 = 3   5 – 2 = 3   (2 + 5 = 7)   7 – 5 = 2

6 – 4 = 2   (4 + 2 = 6)   6 + 2 = 8   5 – 1 = 4   4 + 5 = 9   (9 – 4 = 5)

For the final section, make sure that children
understand that animals approaching each other
represent addition and animals moving away from
each other represent subtraction.

Picture graphs

Look at this picture graph. Then answer the questions.

Mina's marbles

Clear	● ● ● ●
Blue	● ● ●
Green	● ● ● ●
Red	● ● ●
Yellow	●

How many blue
marbles does Mina have?   3

Does Mina have more
green marbles or yellow marbles?   green

How many marbles
does Mina have in all?   16

Look at this picture graph. Then answer the questions.

Books on Pablo's shelf

Cats	
Sports	
Mysteries	
Cartoons	
Science	

How many science
books does Pablo have?   3

Does he have more books
about cats than mysteries?   no

How many more cartoon books
does he have than mysteries?   2

How many books about
cats and science does he have?   6

Look at this picture graph. Then answer the questions.

Pets on Redmond Road

Cats	
Dogs	
Fish	
Birds	

On Redmond Road,
are there more cats or dogs?   dogs

How many more
fish are there than dogs?   2 more

How many cats
and dogs are there?   9

How many pets are there in all?   19

Children need to count the items for each category,
and then add, subtract, and compare data.

3-dimensional shapes

Write the name of each shape.

sphere   cube

Write the name of each shape. Use the words in the word box.

Word Box
sphere   prism   cone   cube   cylinder   pyramid

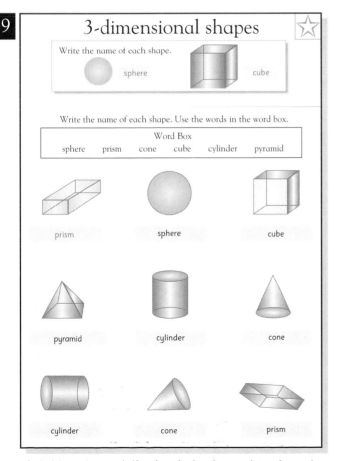

prism   sphere   cube

pyramid   cylinder   cone

cylinder   cone   prism

If children have difficulty, help them identify each
shape and learn its name.

Missing addends

Write the missing addend.

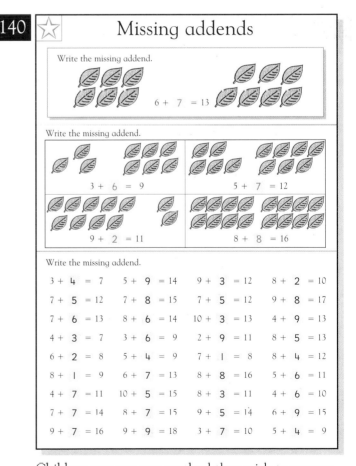

6 + 7 = 13

Write the missing addend.

3 + 6 = 9   5 + 7 = 12

9 + 2 = 11   8 + 8 = 16

Write the missing addend.

3 + 4 = 7	5 + 9 = 14	9 + 3 = 12	8 + 2 = 10
7 + 5 = 12	7 + 8 = 15	7 + 5 = 12	9 + 8 = 17
7 + 6 = 13	8 + 6 = 14	10 + 3 = 13	4 + 9 = 13
4 + 3 = 7	3 + 6 = 9	2 + 9 = 11	8 + 5 = 13
6 + 2 = 8	5 + 4 = 9	7 + 1 = 8	8 + 4 = 12
8 + 1 = 9	6 + 7 = 13	8 + 8 = 16	5 + 6 = 11
4 + 7 = 11	10 + 5 = 15	8 + 3 = 11	4 + 6 = 10
7 + 7 = 14	8 + 7 = 15	9 + 5 = 14	6 + 9 = 15
9 + 7 = 16	9 + 9 = 18	3 + 7 = 10	5 + 4 = 9

Children can use any method they wish to answer
these problems—using related subtraction facts,
counting, or number sense. They should be able
to complete the page using mental math.

Reading tables

Read the table. Then answer the questions.

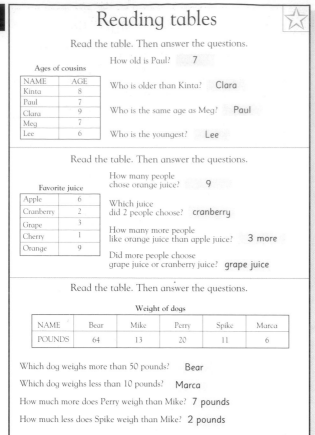

Ages of cousins

NAME	AGE
Kinta	8
Paul	7
Clara	9
Meg	7
Lee	6

How old is Paul?   **7**

Who is older than Kinta?   **Clara**

Who is the same age as Meg?   **Paul**

Who is the youngest?   **Lee**

Read the table. Then answer the questions.

Favorite juice

Apple	6
Cranberry	2
Grape	3
Cherry	1
Orange	9

How many people chose orange juice?   **9**

Which juice did 2 people choose?   **cranberry**

How many more people like orange juice than apple juice?   **3 more**

Did more people choose grape juice or cranberry juice?   **grape juice**

Read the table. Then answer the questions.

Weight of dogs

NAME	Bear	Mike	Perry	Spike	Marca
POUNDS	64	13	20	11	6

Which dog weighs more than 50 pounds?   **Bear**

Which dog weighs less than 10 pounds?   **Marca**

How much more does Perry weigh than Mike?   **7 pounds**

How much less does Spike weigh than Mike?   **2 pounds**

If children have difficulty reading the information in the last table, help them with one question, reading across the appropriate row and down the appropriate column, showing them the intersection of the two.

Adding

Write the answer in the box.

34	26	73
+ 13	+ 15	+ 27
47	41	100

Write the answer in the box.

45	31	53	62
+ 24	+ 18	+ 26	+ 16
69	49	79	78

37	26	72	45
+ 10	+ 13	+ 15	+ 24
47	39	87	69

39	24	52	36
+ 10	+ 15	+ 17	+ 13
49	39	69	49

56	12	67	54
+ 14	+ 16	+ 11	+ 16
70	28	78	70

48	64	36	55
+ 12	+ 14	+ 13	+ 15
60	78	49	70

26	37	48	56
+ 17	+ 14	+ 19	+ 17
43	51	67	73

28	64	56	38
+ 16	+ 26	+ 27	+ 23
44	90	83	61

29	37	28	19
+ 24	+ 27	+ 17	+ 26
53	64	45	45

26	36	46	34
+ 38	+ 76	+ 44	+ 66
64	112	90	100

Most of the sums require regrouping. Make sure that children do not neglect to add 10 to the tens column when they regroup.

Reading a calendar

Look at this calendar. Then answer the questions.

September

S	M	T	W	T	F	S
	1	2	3	4	5	6
7	8	9	10	11	12	13
14	15	16	17	18	19	20
21	22	23	24	25	26	27
28	29	30				

What day of the week is the first day of September on this calendar?   **Monday**

What date is the last Tuesday in September?   **September 30**

Look at this calendar. Then answer the questions.

July

S	M	T	W	T	F	S
				1	2	3
4	5	6	7	8	9	10
11	12	13	14	15	16	17
18	19	20	21	22	23	24
25	26	27	28	29	30	31

How many days are in the month of July?   **31 days**

What day of the week is the last day of July on this calendar?   **Saturday**

A camp starts on July 5 and ends on July 9. How many camp days are there?   **5 days**

The campers go swimming on Tuesday and Thursday. On which dates will they swim?   **July 6 and July 8**

Look at this calendar. Then answer the questions.

November

S	M	T	W	T	F	S
						1
2	3	4	5	6	7	8
9	10	11	12	13	14	15
16	17	18	19	20	21	22
23	24	25	26	27	28	29
30						

What date is the first Sunday of November?   **November 2**

What day of the week is November 14?   **Friday**

How many Saturdays are shown in November?   **5**

Jenna's birthday is November 23. What day of the week is it?   **Sunday**

If children have difficulties, make sure they understand the abbreviations used in the calendars, and are able to read the calendars accurately.

Subtracting

Write the answer in the box.

73	45	72
− 48	− 26	− 36
25	19	36

Write the answer in the box.

67	43	63	72
− 48	− 26	− 46	− 45
19	17	17	27

71	82	63	90
− 47	− 36	− 44	− 47
24	46	19	43

80	90	65	81
− 46	− 63	− 37	− 47
34	27	28	34

Write the answer in the box.

46 in.	59 in.	74 in.	60 in.
− 18 in.	− 36 in.	− 27 in.	− 44 in.
28 in.	23 in.	47 in.	16 in.

70 in.	54 in.	39 in.	91 in.
− 47 in.	− 26 in.	− 4 in.	− 47 in.
23 in.	28 in.	35 in.	44 in.

Write the answer in the box.

43¢	61¢	73¢	71¢
− 17¢	− 24¢	− 36¢	− 46¢
26¢	37¢	37¢	25¢

70¢	81¢	63¢	74¢
− 44¢	− 37¢	− 46¢	− 44¢
26¢	44¢	17¢	30¢

90 in.	94 in.	96 in.	98 in.
− 34 in.	− 47 in.	− 78 in.	− 45 in.
56 in.	47 in.	18 in.	53 in.

Most of the subtraction exercises require regrouping. Make sure children remember to regroup correctly.

Properties of polygons

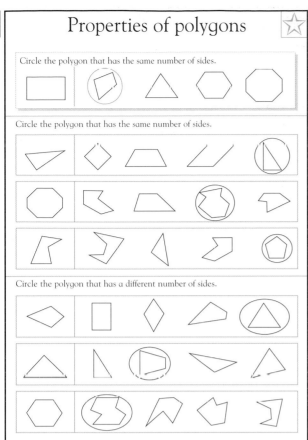

Circle the polygon that has the same number of sides.

Circle the polygon that has the same number of sides.

Circle the polygon that has a different number of sides.

Make sure that children understand that they are not looking for identical shapes, but figures with the given number of sides.

Venn diagrams

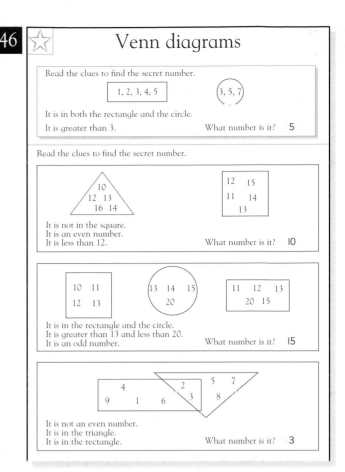

Read the clues to find the secret number.

1, 2, 3, 4, 5   3, 5, 7

It is in both the rectangle and the circle.
It is greater than 3.   What number is it?   5

Read the clues to find the secret number.

10
12 13
16 14

12 15
11 14
13

It is not in the square.
It is an even number.
It is less than 12.   What number is it?   10

10 11
12 13

13 14 15
20

11 12 13
20 15

It is in the rectangle and the circle.
It is greater than 13 and less than 20.
It is an odd number.   What number is it?   15

4   2   5 7
9   1   6   3   8

It is not an even number.
It is in the triangle.
It is in the rectangle.   What number is it?   3

If children have difficulties, "walk" them through the example. The final question is a Venn diagram showing which numbers are in both figures. You may want to ask children which numbers are in both the triangle and the rectangle.

Most likely/least likely

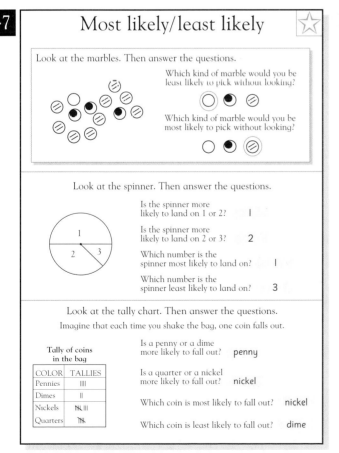

Look at the marbles. Then answer the questions.

Which kind of marble would you be least likely to pick without looking?

Which kind of marble would you be most likely to pick without looking?

Look at the spinner. Then answer the questions.

Is the spinner more likely to land on 1 or 2?   1

Is the spinner more likely to land on 2 or 3?   2

Which number is the spinner most likely to land on?   1

Which number is the spinner least likely to land on?   3

Look at the tally chart. Then answer the questions.
Imagine that each time you shake the bag, one coin falls out.

Tally of coins in the bag

COLOR	TALLIES
Pennies	IIII
Dimes	II
Nickels	ЖЖ III
Quarters	ЖЖ

Is a penny or a dime more likely to fall out?   penny

Is a quarter or a nickel more likely to fall out?   nickel

Which coin is most likely to fall out?   nickel

Which coin is least likely to fall out?   dime

Children should realize that the more of a particular item there is in a set, the more likely it is to be picked.

3-dimensional shapes

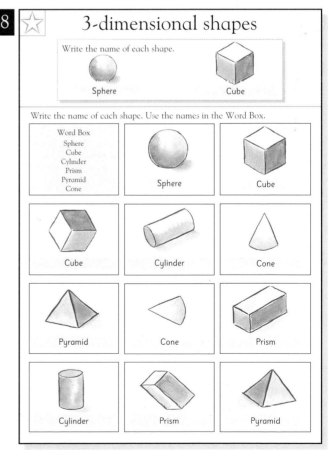

Write the name of each shape.

Sphere   Cube

Write the name of each shape. Use the names in the Word Box.

Word Box
Sphere
Cube
Cylinder
Prism
Pyramid
Cone

Sphere   Cube

Cube   Cylinder   Cone

Pyramid   Cone   Prism

Cylinder   Prism   Pyramid

Children may confuse figures that have an unusual orientation. You may want to use real objects to help demonstrate this.

Counting

Write the missing number above each ↑.

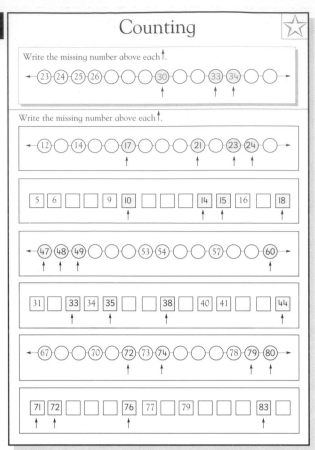

←(23)(24)(25)(26)( )( )( )(30)( )( )(33)(34)( )( )→

Write the missing number above each ↑.

←(12)( )(14)( )(17)( )( )( )(21)( )(23)(24)( )→

| 5 | 6 | | | 9 | 10 | | | | 14 | 15 | 16 | | 18 |

←(47)(48)(49)( )( )( )(53)(54)( )( )(57)( )( )(60)→

| 31 | | 33 | 34 | 35 | | | 38 | | 40 | 41 | | | 44 |

←(67)( )( )(70)( )(72)(73)(74)( )( )( )(78)(79)(80)→

| 71 | 72 | | | | 76 | 77 | | 79 | | | | 83 | |

Each of the sequences involves counting by 1s. Children should fill in only the shapes marked with an arrow.

Finding patterns

Find the counting pattern. Write the missing numbers.

| 12 | 14 | 16 | 18 | 20 | 22 | 24 | 26 | 28 | 30 |

Find the counting pattern. Write the missing numbers.

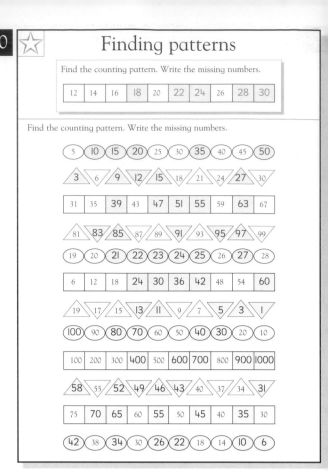

(5)(10)(15)(20)(25)(30)(35)(40)(45)(50)

(3)(6)(9)(12)(15)(18)(21)(24)(27)(30)

| 31 | 35 | 39 | 43 | 47 | 51 | 55 | 59 | 63 | 67 |

(81)(83)(85)(87)(89)(91)(93)(95)(97)(99)

(19)(20)(21)(22)(23)(24)(25)(26)(27)(28)

| 6 | 12 | 18 | 24 | 30 | 36 | 42 | 48 | 54 | 60 |

(19)(17)(15)(13)(11)(9)(7)(5)(3)(1)

(100)(90)(80)(70)(60)(50)(40)(30)(20)(10)

| 100 | 200 | 300 | 400 | 500 | 600 | 700 | 800 | 900 | 1000 |

(58)(55)(52)(49)(46)(43)(40)(37)(34)(31)

| 75 | 70 | 65 | 60 | 55 | 50 | 45 | 40 | 35 | 30 |

(42)(38)(34)(30)(26)(22)(18)(14)(10)(6)

It may be necessary to point out that some of the patterns show an increase and some a decrease. Children can see what operation turns a number into the next number in the pattern, and then perform the operation to continue the pattern.

Reading tally charts

Look at the tally chart. Then answer the questions.

Winners at Tag

Kelly	Mark	Sandy	Rita	Brad
JHT II	III	JHT I	IIII	JHT IIII

Who won the most games? Brad

Who won more games, Sandy or Kelly? Kelly

How many more games did Rita win than Mark? 2 more

Look at the tally chart. Then answer the questions.

Colors of T-Shirts sold

Blue	JHT JHT I
White	JHT III
Green	JHT IIII
Black	JHT JHT II

Which color shirt was sold most? black

How many green shirts were sold? 9

Which color sold more, blue or green? blue

How many black shirts were sold? 12

How many more green shirts were sold than white shirts? 1 more

How many more black shirts were sold than green shirts? 3 more

How many T-shirts were sold in all? 40

Look at the tally chart. Then answer the questions.

Snack choices

Chips	Cherries	Cheese	Cookie	Apple
JHT IIII	JHT	JHT JHT I	JHT III	JHT II

How many people chose chips? 9

Which snack did 7 people choose? apple

Did more people choose chips or cookies? chips

Which snack did the fewest people choose? cherries

How many more people chose cheese than chips? 2 more

How many people chose apples and cherries? 12

Children usually accept the concept of tally marks very quickly. They can count on by fives for completed tallies.

Same shape and size

Which figure has same shape and size?

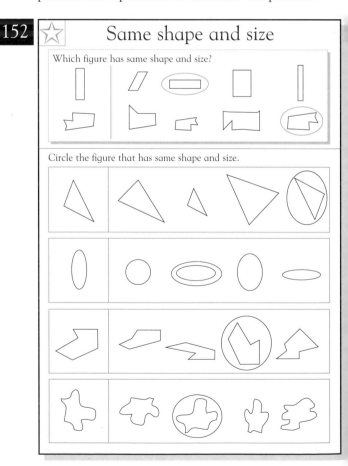

Circle the figure that has same shape and size.

Make sure children look for both size and shape. They may have difficulty if the figures are drawn with different orientations.

Parts of a set

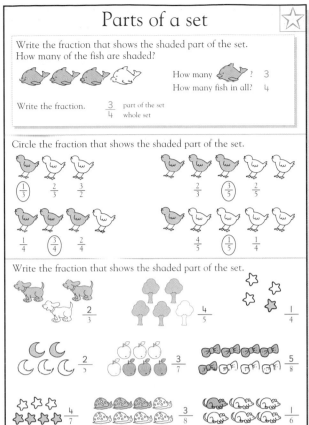

Write the fraction that shows the shaded part of the set.
How many of the fish are shaded?

How many 🐟 ? 3
How many fish in all? 4

Write the fraction. $\frac{3}{4}$ part of the set
whole set

Circle the fraction that shows the shaded part of the set.

$\frac{1}{3}$ $\frac{2}{3}$ $\frac{3}{2}$ $\frac{2}{3}$ $\frac{3}{5}$ $\frac{2}{5}$

$\frac{1}{4}$ $\frac{3}{4}$ $\frac{2}{4}$ $\frac{4}{5}$ $\frac{1}{5}$ $\frac{1}{4}$

Write the fraction that shows the shaded part of the set.

$\frac{2}{3}$ $\frac{4}{5}$ $\frac{1}{4}$

$\frac{2}{5}$ $\frac{3}{7}$ $\frac{5}{8}$

$\frac{4}{7}$ $\frac{3}{8}$ $\frac{1}{6}$

If children have difficulties, point out that the denominator—or bottom number of the fraction—is the total number of parts. The numerator—or top part of the fraction—is the number of shaded parts.

Symmetry

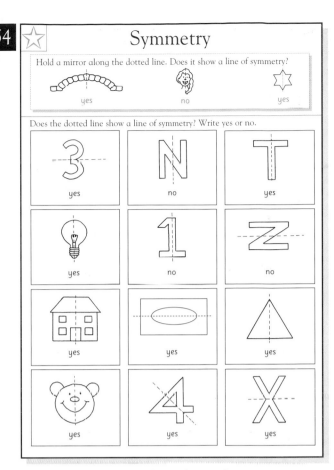

Hold a mirror along the dotted line. Does it show a line of symmetry?

yes   no   yes

Does the dotted line show a line of symmetry? Write yes or no.

3	N	T
yes	no	yes
💡	1	Z
yes	no	no
🏠	⬭	△
yes	yes	yes
🐻	4	X
yes	yes	yes

Some of these shapes have lines of symmetry in unusual positions. Let children use mirrors on the shapes if they are unsure of their answers.

Measurement problems

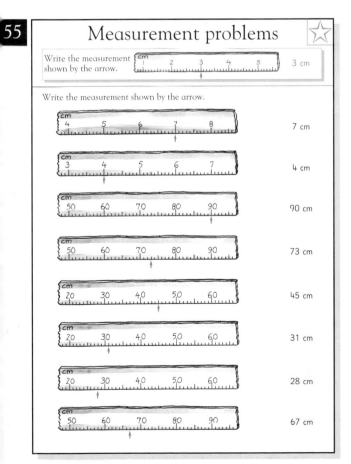

Write the measurement shown by the arrow.   3 cm

Write the measurement shown by the arrow.

7 cm

4 cm

90 cm

73 cm

45 cm

31 cm

28 cm

67 cm

Children should be able to read off scales of this type relatively easily. Make sure that children include the units in their answers.

3-dimensional shapes

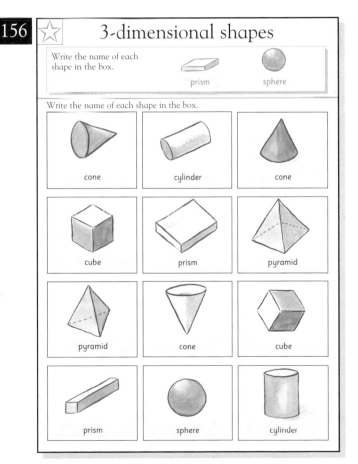

Write the name of each shape in the box.   prism   sphere

Write the name of each shape in the box.

cone	cylinder	cone
cube	prism	pyramid
pyramid	cone	cube
prism	sphere	cylinder

Children may be uncertain of the terms *prism* and *pyramid*. Show them objects to demonstrate the difference.